God you are such a blessing to me!

May God Bless You Greatly

minister Gregory Johnson

No More
DISTRACTIONS

No More
DISTRACTIONS

Written By: Gregory D. Johnson

Dominion Publishing
Baltimore, MD

Unless otherwise indicated, scripture quotations are from the Holy Bible, King James Bible, New International Version®, NIV ®, Copyright © 1973, 1978, 1984, 2011 by Biblica, Inc. ™ Webster Dictionary and www.Dictionary.com, Quotations from, Dr. Myles Munroe, Prophet Mike Coates, Minister Shawnta Clark, Pastor Mark Batterson, Dr. Andre Lynch.

For more information about the title, please contact:

Dominion Publishing
www.gregdjohnson.net
Baltimore, MD
printgreg@yahoo.com

Book Cover designed by:

Mr. Gregory D. Johnson

Printed in the United States

ISBN-10:1505221803

Dedication

I dedicate this book to my champions in heaven who are rooting me on to be all that I was created to be; to my father, the one and only Jesus Christ himself; my Grandmother, the late Josephine Ellen Johnson; my Grandfather, the late Frank E. Henderson; my God Mother, the late Evangelist Joan C. Spence; my Auntie, the late Minister Bettie Mae Crandol; and My Mentor, The late Rev. Dr. Gerald Weiss.

I also dedicate this book to my mother, Christine E. Henderson; my father, Gregory D. Johnson Sr.; my grandmother, Helen R. Jones; my grandfather, John (Shelia) Jordan; my second parents, Nancy M. & Robert L. Wallace; my spiritual parents, Elder Chris & Pastor Jekia Ledbetter; my pastor & spiritual father, Bishop Cornelius Showell & First Lady Augusta Showell; all of my siblings; My cousins, Kendra & Eugene McIntyre; my twin aunts, Linda Cash and Brenda Tilghman; my God-children, Jaylin, Brenden, Jajuan, Ava, Jaidah, Brianna and Dominique Jr.; my godfather, Antiono Spence; to my destiny partners and confidants, Dr. Jovan Walker, Prophet Michael Coates, Minister Bernard (Shelia) Briggs, Minister Adam Turnage, Sister Cynthia Porcher, Brother Michael (Tia) Robinson, and Minister Anthony Fletcher; to my mentees: Minister James S. McBride, Minister Ke'Andre R. Lucas, Minister Jazmyn Ledbetter and Minister David Lee; to my god-sisters, Shannah Hughes, Mone't Horton and Pastor Arlethia (Larry) Jones; to the greatest aunties in the world, Minister Charlene Fitch, Minister Peggy Williams and Elder Sharon S. Green; to every young man (past & present) at the Maryland Department of Juvenile Services in Baltimore, MD. I dedicate this book to all of my Shortline kids past and present, co-workers and to my over 300 grandparents at the Charlestown Retirement Community.

Acknowledgements and Thanks

I would like to take this time to acknowledge and honor some of the greatest people on the planet, those who have impacted my life in a tremendous way. To my uncle, Elder John Hancock, Pastor Stephany Graham (Peekskill, New York), Pastor Anthony Scott, and Elder Sheri Rowson, Pastors Keith and Saundra Holley, Bishop Timothy Cuffia and the late First Lady Francis Cuffia, Pastor Issac & Mother Freddie Mae Joy (Momma), Elder Barbara Johnson, Pastor Roderick (Nadia) Smith, Apostle Damian (Cheryl) Hinton, Apostle Dwight Smith, and Elder Tina Kane.

To my instructors: Elder Emmanuel Vaughn, Elder Melvina Wilson, Elder Lenora Showell, Elder Lawerence Greene, Elder Curtis (Sonya) Eaddy, Elder Beatrice Hopkins, Elder André Lynch, Elder Diane Fitzhugh, Dr. Harold Hart, Dr. Joseph Raddine and Dr. Charles Olukun from Morgan State University. To my brothers and sisters in ministry: Minister Marlin (Tiffany) Austin, Elder Aaron Wilson, Minister Zeshara Cosby, Minister Tinya Kent, Minister Shawnta M. Clark, Minister Dominque (Loren) Chandler, Minister Larry Stevenson, Minister Shirley Crews, Minister Lydia Carter, Minister Doris Smith, Brother Parry Long, Brother Henry Burt, Minister Keyona Waddell, Elder Shirley Lewis, Elder Johnnie and Minister Loretta Sharp, Minister C. Ralph, Ministers Patrick & Cherie Brown, Minister Fred Scott, Minister Cornell Showell, Sister Natalie Johnson, Pastor Wayne Lee, Elder Charline Bethea, Elder Denise Morgan, and Minister Deborah Bryant. To Ms. Susanne Maennik Ridenour from St. Mary's Seminary & University for her generous support and encouragement. To my co-workers and greatest friends: Mariah (Kevin) Roy, Breyon Preston, David Haskins, John Christensen, Scott Woods, and Frederica Joy. Special thanks to Sister Glenda Freeman, Brother Gregory Chew, Mother Alice Coates, to my brothers, Chris, Craig, Tyrell, and Travis, and to my sisters, Shenika, Breonna, and Kierra. To my best friend from childhood Ambrosia Collins-Conway (Tony), and to my greatest friends, Leah, Shannon, Zack, Katrice, Chanel, Teryn, Chantel, and La'Ren. To Ms. Estelle and Mr. Ocey Harris, Deacon Levi and Trustee Frederica Coates, Deacon Clarence and Trustee Erica Brown, Ms. Hazel and Mr. Jack Seal, Angitha, Zecia, Sabrina Scott, and Amina Pleasant-bey, Princess Je'Layah Ledbetter and to my esteemed editor, Dr. Eugenia Collier (Morgan State University); Special thanks to my esteemed co-editors and proof readers, Sister Zoann Mouzone and Minister Zeshara Cosby; My entire First Apostolic Faith Church, Victory Ministries of Christ Church, Kingdom Nation Church & Ministries, Greater Manifestation Worship and Praise Ministry, Divine Mission Apostolic and Deliverance and Healing Center families. To all of my aunts, uncles, cousins and friends I love each of you.

Contents

Introduction

"Get ready; prepare yourself to live a life that's Undistracted."

Introduction

Great blessings to you. I am super excited that you are holding "No More Distractions" in your hands. It's certainly not by happenstance that this book has found its way into your precious hands. It's my firm belief that God has ordained this book to be written, edited, printed, mailed, shipped, purchased or given to you for such a time as this. It's my prayer that at first glimpse of the cover, the Holy Spirit will lead you to dive into the pages of this book. I have blessed and prayed over this book that it would fall into the hands of the right person and that person beloved, is YOU!

In a world where there are so many distractions, we often lose focus of our goals and our missions, only to realize years later that we have become victims of distractions that have hindered us from moving forward in our dreams, missions and goals. However, there is a place in our lives where we can live a fulfilled, focused, driven life that is undistracted. I charge you through this book to recognize and eliminate any of the distractions that get in your way. The distractions that seek to hinder and stifle you from moving forward in your purpose and in your destiny.

Beloved, get ready! Prepare yourself! To live a life that's undistracted. I dare you to declare: "No More Distractions!" Now give our God some praise for every distraction that has just left your life at the command of your decree.

Chapter I

Jesus, Mary & Martha

Chapter I,
Jesus, Mary & Martha

"But Martha was distracted by all the preparations that had to be made. She came to him and asked, "Lord, don't you care that my sister has left me to do the work by myself? Tell her to help me!" – Luke 10:40 (NIV)

We live in a society where there are so many distractions. Each and every day we will encounter one distraction or another. Whether we are driving to work, sitting in the classroom at school or listening to the sermon at church, distractions are everywhere. In a time where technology, texting and social media have caused so many to be impersonal, unsociable and unaware that sometimes we lose who we really are and miss some of life's most precious moments. We can become so caught up in the busyness of our lives and our daily routines that we miss many of the miracles and precious moments that have presented themselves in our lives. We often get so caught up in a life that's distracted that we don't savor the moments, miracles, people and things that matter. Our greatest miracle could be standing right before us or may have just entered our lives, but because we were so distracted we didn't recognize it. I dare you to take this moment and appreciate it, for God has pulled you away from the distractions surrounding you just to get your attention.

Before we dive into such a great story in Luke Chapter 10, May I pose a few questions to you? Can you first forget about your problems? Can you forget about the noise that's going on all around you? Can you forget about the noise and commotion that's going on in your head? Can you forget about the problems that are awaiting you moments after you place this book down? Can you give God your full, undivided, uninterrupted, undistracted attention? God is speaking and all He ever wanted was for you to take time out to listen. It's a fact that although you haven't been listening to Him, He's still been speaking. He has just been speaking over top of all of the noise. You just couldn't hear Him because of the many distractions in your life at the moment. I dare you before you go any farther into this book that you, turn your television off, log out of all of social media accounts, get in a quiet place, lift your hands in worship and surrender and begin to worship the father in spirit and in truth. Put something sweet on your lips about Him ("Lord we worship you, we adore you, we lift you up, you are our God and beside you there is no other......) Amen.

We see in chapter 10 of Luke that Jesus and many of His disciples are traveling and headed to Jerusalem to spread the good news of the kingdom of God. Jesus sends the seventy out two by two and commissions them to preach the gospel wherever they are sent and if they find no peace in that place, they are to kick the dust off of their feet and keep moving. While traveling they were invited into the home of a woman named Martha who hosted one of Jesus' random teaching and impartation sessions. Jesus and His disciples are on a mission to spread the gospel of the kingdom and they are having these in modern day terms mini-town hall meeting sessions in the homes of devout believer's. In those days the Church were not huge cathedrals with theatre seats, bright lights, microphones and a praise and worship team. The church was a group of believers who gathered to hear the unfolding and the unveiling of the Holy Scriptures. The church was where ever they resided, if it was on the countryside, that's where they had church, if it was in the middle of the sea that's where they had church and in this case they have church in the home of a woman whose name is Martha.

Martha was the hostess and Jesus was the very special guest. We must note that Martha didn't have just anybody in her home; she had the opportunity and privilege to entertain the King of kings and the Lord of lords. Beloved, she has God represented in the flesh standing in the family room of her home. How exciting this must have been for Martha to have had in her home the lamb that was slain before the foundation of the world. I could just imagine how Jesus' very presence transformed her home into a temple or a dwelling place it made it sacred and holy. I could imagine the anxiety that she possessed because she wanted his visit to be perfect.

Martha understands the art of hospitality and her duties as a hostess and a woman. However, Martha becomes so consumed and determined to make sure that the meal and service provided to Jesus and His guest were perfect and extremely fit for them, that she neglects Him. She doesn't take full advantage of the fact that dwelling with her is the word that became flesh. Because of her "much" serving, she becomes so distracted, pulled away or absorbed by her many duties that she never becomes a partaker of the "Rhema" that's proceeding out of the mouth of our Lord and Savior Jesus Christ. On the other hand, her sister Mary, who was once in the kitchen preparing the same meal with her, leaves and sits at the feet of Jesus and listens to His teachings. Mary assumes the posture of humility and humbleness, the posture of a student or disciple. For a woman to sit among men or sit at the feet of a Rabbi (teacher) at this period of time was uncommon and rather unorthodox. For only men sat at the feet of the teacher during those times, as did Paul, who sat at the feet of Gamaliel, a highly respected teacher of the law. This struck a nerve in Martha and it upset her. Maybe Martha felt as though Mary was acting in the place of a man or that she was out of place. However, Mary's stance and position shakes the very foundation of Martha's traditional distorted view of the role of women who followed Jesus. And it's in this instance that Mary brings liberation for women believers.

It is this Mary who chooses to be focused and undistracted. Mary, who doesn't say a single word in the text, has the loudest voice in the text because she positions herself to receive, breaks tradition and liberates women to be public disciples of Jesus. She chooses to listen; she left the noise, the busyness and the commotion to receive the right now word from the Lord. Her position is that of an undistracted, focused servant of the most-high God, who is expecting to receive something from the master. Mary understands what Jesus says in Mathew 4:4, "that man shall not live by bread alone but by every word that comes out of the mouth of God."

I dare you to take the position and posture of Mary today. Stop what you are doing, put down this book, and press your ear until you hear the master; He is speaking a word concerning you at this very moment. God can speak a word that has the ability to transform your life for the rest of your life. All you need is one word from God and it can shift your entire life. God was waiting for this book to find you so He could get your attention and tell you why you were created and what He needs you to do. He tried so many other times, with different instances but to no avail: there were too many people around you, too much music playing in your ears and too many things for you to do. But today is your day. He has your full undivided attention. When the student is ready the teacher will appear. Are you ready?

While Mary has assumed this posture of receiving, her sister Martha makes a complaint to Jesus in verse 40 that He doesn't care that Mary has left her alone to serve by herself. She suggests to Jesus that He should bid Mary to come back and help her. However Jesus' response to her was sort of an indictment, for He says, "Martha chooses to be pulled away from the essential thing." This essential thing has been choked out by well-intended over-activity. He says that Martha is troubled by many things or distracted by much. In other words her good intentions have gotten her into the place of being distracted. He implores her to focus on the one important thing, which is himself and the word of God. He tells her that she should take on one task at a time. We must often remind ourselves that it's not the number of things that we do for God that pleases Him but rather how well we accomplish each task for Him successfully. We should pursue each task for Him one by one, accomplish it, and move on to the next.

Beloved, many times we become so busy doing work for the Lord that we never get a chance to encounter Him. We can become so busy serving Him that we miss Him. What is it to have served the Lord all of our lives and yet have no relationship with Him? What is it to be employed by God but never talk with Him or even listen to what He has to say? Our God is yet speaking and He's waiting for someone to listen. The entire time that Martha was preparing the meal, Jesus was still speaking; she was just not in the position to hear

Him. There was too much to do, there was too much noise and commotion, there was too much work to do for Him, there was a meal that needed to be prepared. However, Martha didn't realize that He really didn't need food, because He was the very bread out of heaven, and that He was a spring of living water and the well that never ran dry. Beloved, she was so concerned about meeting the needs of Jesus that she missed the fact that Jesus came to supply her needs, He came to break her traditional mindset, and He came to offer the kingdom to all that would believe.

Jesus was passing by and Martha missed her moment. She didn't seize the moment. My brother or my sister, if Jesus enters into the room right now! Would you know what to do? Would you stop what you were doing just to listen to Him? Would you revere His very presence? Would you stop and listen? Would you seize the moment? Would you even recognize His presence? Can you put yourself to the side and all that you need, and all that you are going through right now and just bask in His presence?

Many times we get so caught up in our lives that we no longer have time for God. Our lives have become too complicated, but what is a life without God at the dead center of it? Is there any fulfillment? Is there any sense of purpose? For the bible tells us that without Him we are nothing, but in Him we can do all things.

We must remember that even in our serving God we can overdo it and accomplish nothing. I call this unproductive busyness, when we work, work, work, serve, serve, serve and in turn there is nothing to show for it. We become frustrated and upset and begin to feel abandoned, rejected and empty. Unfortunately this is the testimony of many and is an indication that everybody that says they working for the Lord isn't productive. There are individuals who have put their work in the name of Jesus but actually don't have Him in mind at all.

We must pull away as Jesus did to get instructions for the rest of our journey. Our work and serving must be validated by God for it to be official and meaningful. We must get to the place where we don't allow our busyness to distract us. My brother or my sister slow down and take time out for God. The Bible declares that the steps of a good man (woman) are ordered by God and if we are going to go to our next dimension in God and be effective we must take time out to hear from Him. And listen to what He has to say.

Jesus lastly addresses the power of choice. What we must understand today is that God has equipped all of us with the power and ability to choose. This can be traced back to the Garden of Eden and we see it throughout scripture that God never takes our right to choose away. Jesus states to Martha the thing that is needful and He calls it good. He says the gospel is needful, the word of God is needful and relationship with Him is needful. In order for us to serve effectively we must make the conscious decision to be focused and undistracted. Beloved, when we make that decision we won't have to speak for ourselves, because the master will speak for us in our circumstances. He'll assure us that our focus will not be taken away. The devil may try, but you'll be protected. I dare you to keep your mouth closed and stay focused on the master and the task that He has placed into your hands and you'll receive everything that you need. There are some dreams that you must fulfill, some visions that you haven't written down yet, some degrees to earn, some books to write, a business to start, a wedding to plan and an assignment to fulfill. It's your time to become undistracted.

Chapter II

A Distracted Life

Chapter II
A Distracted Life

What does a distracted life look like? A distracted life is defined by me as a life that's been drawn away from its intended purpose. We all have been victims of lives that were distracted. We have also witnessed others whose lives were distracted. A distracted life is one that doesn't have meaning. It's a life that has been pulled into the mundane routines of everyday living, where every ounce of that life has become entangled in an endless cycle of distraction. It's in this cycle that you've lost your sense of self-worth and who you were created to be. Where you have become so consumed by the distractions that life has presented to you that you have lost sight of your God ordained purpose and have begun to settle for the lesser purposes instead of the promises that God has made to you.

A distracted life is a life that has lost focus of its purpose. There are so many people who have bought into the distractions of this life that their lives are in disarray, they are frustrated, they feel alone and they haven't accomplished anything. A distracted life is one with regrets. Those should haves! Could haves! Would haves! Many of us who have focused on should haves, could haves, and would haves of our lives have worked themselves into this downward spiral of defeat, having bought into the false notion that there is absolutely no way out.

Life comes with many distractions and for many of us the distractions have won and have taken over our lives. I have admired some of the greatest individuals and have always wondered why so many successful, highly respected and well-known individuals reach the peaks of their careers and of their ministries and then fall. I've often wondered what was it that made them come tumbling down, soon to find out that somewhere on their journey they became distracted. I've also wondered why some of the smartest, most brilliant and talented people succumb to being stuck in the same place year after year. After talking with many of them I've found out that they were distracted by the fear of greatness, success and the unknown. Some even attested to the fact that they were afraid of failure. Being afraid is definitely a distraction that prevents many of us from going forward.

I've also learned that even focused people at some time or another will become distracted and lose their focus. I liken it to a man or woman who is driving a car. He or she sets out to an attended destination, but on the road to the destination there are so many distractions that seek to hinder that person from making it to the destination on time.

It's the objective of the distractions on your road to destiny to hinder you from arriving at all. Beloved, we must be very careful of the distractions on the road to destiny that seeks to derail and delay our destinies. There are so many distractions that have caused us to pull over to the side of the road or have caused us to get off on the wrong exit and detour from our intended paths; and unfortunately we have been on this detour for years trying to find our way back to our God-ordained paths. For many of us this has left us riding in circles wasting precious time, resources and energy in a place going nowhere. I would rather be sitting in slow moving traffic going 5mph then off on a detour not even close to my destination. If we are going to make it to our destination, we must learn to be patient even when it doesn't feel like we are making progress.

Another reason that slows us down on our road to destiny is being distracted by what others are doing (Minding someone else's business). There are many times that I drive the highway, and often traffic is very slow. As I get closer to my destination it appears that there are police lights flashing on the side of the road. While I am driving I'm assuming that there must be an accident that is delaying traffic, only to find out that there was no accident but merely someone who has been pulled over for some reason or another and the delay of the traffic is only because the persons driving the cars in front of me are trying to figure out the reason the police are there. This delay in traffic is caused by a traffic term called rubber-necking. Rubbernecking is ones interest in someone else's business or affairs. We must get to the place where we stop being distracted by what others are doing and actually focus on what we are supposed to be doing. For many of us we have become so concerned with what our brother or our sister is doing and their short comings that we lose focus of our own lives and we become active participants in rubber-necking. I often say that we have so much to do and fix in our own lives that there isn't enough time to worry about someone else's.

Then we have the distraction of what others think and say about us. Never allow what other people say or think about you keep you from focusing. What they say or think doesn't matter. Let them talk and let them keep thinking. You keep focused and realize that they will still be talking and still thinking when you reach your destiny.

I have witnessed family members whose lives have been ruined by distractions. Family members who started out focused but allowed the distractions of drugs, money, partying, past hurts, un-forgiveness, ill spoken words, drinking and self-imprisonment to hinder them from living. I've watched good people be taken down by the distractions of this life. I've seen and watched members of my family succumb to distractions that eventually took their lives. I will never forget growing up as a kid in the lower part of Edmondson Village witnessing a family member overdose on drugs. This was horrifying. The paramedics were called, and they were able to revive him, only to find out moments later that this near-death experience was not enough to stop him from abusing himself with more drugs. As a child I couldn't understand it. Why would someone intentionally want to harm himself to the point of death? But as an adult I truly understand it.

This family member had allowed his life's failures, hurts, bad experiences, feelings of abandonment and shortcomings distract him from living, and every chance he got he tried to escape his reality and instead of dealing with the pain, he in turn self-medicated as a way of escape. Beloved, that's the job of the distraction; its job is to get you to the place of existing instead of living. Its job is to get you to focus on your failures, hurts, bad experiences, feelings of abandonment and shortcomings so you won't live but rather merely exist. For many of us use our distractions as a way of escaping our realities and at the end of the day our realities have not changed.

As a minister I have witnessed many individuals whose lives were filled with distractions. Having ministered to hundreds of individuals throughout my short years of ministering, I have encouraged and prayed for those who have fallen victim to the distractions surrounding them, those who had lost all hope, those who had encountered life's most dreadful experiences and didn't see a way out. I have stood in amazement and witnessed how the word of God brought them back into focus.

The most common place that we are usually distracted is in our minds and in our thinking. That's usually the starting place. What is a distracted mind? It's a mind that has been pulled away from its intended focus to the point of not completing the task. There are so many individuals who are distracted in their minds that they can barely function in everyday life. They are so distracted by internal turmoil that they suffer from insomnia, depression and lack of focus. It's in this instance that the internalized distractions hinder the focus of the person. I once read a story online of a monk who couldn't meditate and focus while at home because of his wife, kids and neighbors, so he decides to go to a forest to meditate. However, when he tries to meditate in the forest, suddenly past memories of loved ones and internal issues begin to bother him, and he eventually decides to go back home to meditate. We must be very conscious of the fact that it's very easy for us to get distracted without an outside influence. Many times it's that internal distraction that causes our thinking to be unfocused.

We must take control of our thoughts. The Bible says in Proverbs 23:7 "for as a man thinks in his heart so is he." We must learn to make our thoughts pay a toll. No thought should ever come to your mind that you don't judge. One of my greatest friends, Prophet Mike Coates, constantly reminds me of this. Our thoughts are powerful and according to the word of God we become our very thoughts. So if you are distracted in your thoughts it will eventually manifest in your physical life. You must remember that any thought that's not adding value to your focus, assignment and purpose is a distraction.

We must take the approach of the word of God to combat the internal distractions in our thinking. The Apostle Paul states in Colossians 3:2, that "we are to set our minds and keep them set on what is above (the higher things), not on the things that are on the earth." He later records in Philippians 4:8, "we must begin to think on the Word or begin to sing a praise song to God. And make a conscious effort to fill our minds with good, pure, wholesome, and lovely thoughts." What are you thinking that's keeping you from focusing? With so much competing for your attention, and so little time to focus, it's a wonder we get anything accomplished at all. Today you must make up your mind that no longer will you allow your life to be distracted by your thoughts and negative thinking. I dare you to declare "No More Distractions."

Chapter III

Good Distractions

Chapter III

Good Distractions

In a world where there are so many bad distractions, let's shift for a moment and focus on the benefits of good distractions. Sometimes we can be so overly engrossed in being focused that we don't have balance. In that case, some occasional distractions would not hurt. Balance for Christians and for focused individuals is very important because an excessive amount of anything even focus is not good for anyone. That's why we interrupt our daily scheduled programming of everyday living and working, and we vacate to the beautiful tropical islands of the Caribbean and other exotic places to shift our focus.

Let us explore some of the benefits of experiencing periods of good distractions. I remember as a college freshman I registered for my freshman English composition course, and I found myself sitting in the classroom of one of the greatest professors that I have ever had the opportunity to encounter. His lectures were very focused and organized; however, he used a very effective and unique teaching method that helped my class mates and me to excel. Guess what he used? He used moments of good distractions. Every 15 minutes in his lecture he would go off subject dead in the middle of his lecture without notice. These good distractions helped the class focus and retain all of the information in his lecture. Later in the semester he revealed his secret as to why his students were so successful in his courses and it totally blew my mind. He apparently did a study of our generation and found out that many if not all of us were accustomed to watching television shows, cartoons and movies when we were younger, and he asked us whether we remembered how in the midst of the show our focus would be interrupted by commercials and later recovered. Many of us stood in amazement and said yes. I stood in awe that this method was so simple but ultimately very powerful. So I began to apply it to my own life.

Focus plus occasional interruption is good. One of my mentors to whom I look up to dearly, Elder André Lynch, sums it up as **"faith + fun = Balance."** He stressed via text one day the importance of enjoying life and embracing that abundant life that Jesus promised and came to give us. I've learned to enjoy and embrace those good distractions that pull me away from my everyday routine so that when I return I can work even harder. In embracing this concept I've made it my business to take a vacation once a year and explore the world. Many times you just need a week or two of clean unplanned fun distractions and relaxation to get you back into focus.

Here is another example of a good distraction. It's in 1 Corinthians 10:13 that states: "There hath no temptation taken you but such as is common to man: but God is faithful, who will not suffer you to be tempted above that ye are able; but will with the temptation also make a way to escape, that ye may be able to bear it." God will provide a way of escape a good distraction. I was sitting in the parking lot of St. Mary's seminary preparing to go into the library. I pulled into my parking space and right smack in front of me there was a "Ford Escape SUV" with the Christian fish and cross emblem on it. So I immediately looked up the meaning of the fish emblem on the internet and it meant Jesus Christ, Son of God, and Savior. Immediately I received the revelation of the way of escape being a good distraction.

There are many times that we may be in situations that we shouldn't or may even be on the verge of committing a sin and the holy spirit will allow a distraction to come that will hinder us from going outside of the will of God. For instance, you may be in the bed, clothes off and getting ready to have sex with a person that you know you shouldn't and the doorbell will ring. You have just encountered a good distraction. You may be about to commit suicide and when you opened the bottle of pills the bottle was empty. You just encountered a good distraction. You were upset because you left the house late because you lost track of time only to find out that on your normal route to work there was a tragic car accident that you know for sure that you could have been in. You just encountered a good distraction. When you were on your way to hell and your mind was far from God, you were given a tract or were invited to come to church and you encountered the presence of God. You heard the good news and you gave Christ your life. You've just encountered a good distraction.

Every now and then we must thank God for the good distractions that He has placed on our paths. For many of us have escaped many things because we adhered to the good distractions that presented themselves to us in the midst of our distress and our sin. The scripture states that God is faithful; if we stop right there we can give God praise, because even when we were not faithful he's been faithful to us. He doesn't send good distractions one time: He does it all the time. He's been faithful unto us because by this we are able to bear any and every thing, person or situation that comes to tempt us.

I am a living witness and recipient of the many good distractions that God has allowed to come into my life. I was headed down a road called "nowhere" and Jesus Christ met me on the road, interrupted my journey, and saved my life. He not only saved me but he delivered me, and then he set me free. We serve an amazing God. I liken it to the story of the Apostle Paul in the book of Acts. Paul was a persecutor of Christians and of God. One day while he was on the road to Damascus his journey was hindered, interrupted and distracted by God. God stopped him dead in his tracks. Paul immediately fell to the ground, and he heard the voice of God. Beloved, Jesus will meet you on the road. It doesn't matter your status or how many credentials that you have or even how much sin you have committed. God will meet you right where you are. God will allow something as simple as a distraction to get your attention.

Scholars say that Saul was knocked off of his beast and this distracted him from persecuting God and Christians anymore. This one distraction changed his life. I have come to realize that there are some testimonies that we will never have because God has distracted, intervened and prevented us from somethings. I often tell the young men that I minister to at the Maryland Department of Juvenile services that God allowed them to get arrested to save their lives. Many if not all of them look at me strangely. In response to their strange look I stress to them that the arrest was a good distraction amongst all of those bad distractions that they were dealing with before they got arrested. For many if not all of them God has warned them time after time to stop being rebellious, or to stop hanging around the wrong people. They didn't always adhere.

So the inevitable happened and they were arrested. Instantly they believe that the arrest is a bad thing. However, I stress to them that God used the arrest to speak to them. He used the very thing that they thought was a bad thing to save their lives both physically and spiritually. He used the arrest to get their attention because they were so distracted. Many of them because they got arrested they escaped death by the skin of their teeth and for the majority of them they received eternal life. It often brings my heart joy when my friends and I go and minister to the young men and they willfully without hesitation give their lives to Christ. This is a beautiful moment that often leaves me in tears and in awe that God's plan is so perfect that he'll save us even from ourselves. I often tell the young men that God will meet you wherever you are. Many times we're looking for him to meet us when everything is going well or we're looking for him to meet us in the church building. But for these young men it's neither of those places. Sunday after Sunday God meets them in a holding cell surrounded by other distracted young men. He meets them through his word and his presence. They come in the door one way and leave another because they encountered a good distraction. His name is Jesus.

God has given to each of us freewill, the ability to choose. At any moment we can choose to override the many ways of escape and good distractions that God allows to distract us from given into temptation, but its then and only then that we will never be able to say that Jesus didn't help us.

Chapter IV

Distractions In Leadership

Chapter IV

Distractions In Church Leadership

One of the greatest tragedies in life is a leader that's distracted and has followers. If you are a leader you must be focused because the people that are following you are expecting you to take them to a place that they can't get to themselves. The reality is that they chose to follow you, because they trust in your leadership and while they know that the road won't be easy, they expect to arrive at their place of destination on time. Whether it's an actual place, a spiritual place or a destination, the leader is responsible for keeping focus because others' lives depend on it.

What is a leader? And after looking up the various definitions of what a leader is I chose this definition stated by Hollander & Julian, 1969 that a leader is "the presence of a particular influence relationship between two or more persons." A leader is an individual who leads or commands a group; it's an individual who enlists the aid and support of others in the accomplishment of a common task to get them to a destination. Leaders are crucial to their followers and in the words of one of my favorite authors, Dr. Myles Munroe

"Being a Leader is not a right, but it is a privilege given by the followers." As leaders we must be very mindful of the distractions on our roads to destiny because the people that are following us gave us that privilege to lead them.

I'm often puzzled at the fact of how successful and effective leaders who have invested their entire lives into being successful leaders suddenly fall by the wayside. I often ponder on what brought them down, only to find out that the answer to that question can be traced back to many distractions. As a leader myself I'm often bombarded with many distractions as I lead. And I have come to understand that distractions are a tool that the devil uses to hinder the process, delay the journey or stop the task from being completed. The enemy hopes to keep the leader and his followers from fulfilling the vision, completing the assignment and being obedient to God. So often leaders have been found in breach of allowing the many distractions that surround them to cloud their vision and to get them unfocused and at the end of the day those who follow them suffer. I have read and seen leaders of Fortune 500 companies become distracted by the greed of money and their corporations collapse and the very ones that trusted in their leadership suffered the consequences of their distractions.

Distractions in leadership are real and must be dealt with by the leader so that the followers will not suffer. The detriments to the followers are many times severe. Whether the leader has 5 followers or 5,000 followers, the consequences can be great.

Let's take a look at the distractions in leadership in the church arena. There is an importance of listening to God. Just because you haven't been listening to him, doesn't change the fact that he's been speaking. He has just been speaking over top of all of the noise, clutter and commotion in your life. You just couldn't hear him.

There are three areas in which a leader in the church must never be distracted, or the leader takes the risk of leading the followers astray:

1. They should never be distracted in their relationship with God. The church leader must not allow anything to distract or hinder prayer and communion with God because this is vital to the leadership. Their followers are following them as

they follow Christ. So how can you lead a people or direct a people to a place and you yourself haven't sought directions? How can you tell the people of God about a God with whom you haven't been in contact? How can you lead a people if you yourself are not being led? This brings us to the subject of performance without relationship which is one of the biggest distractions in church leadership. Many have been distracted by the applause of the people that they have allowed it push them to perform on stage without first consulting with God.

As a leader how can you tell the people you serve about a God that you haven't talked to? If you are a leader in your local church or a leader on the national level of the church you should not allow anything to hinder your study of God's word.

Next the church leader should not be distracted in their giving of tithes and offerings. Leaders must lead in this commandment of scripture so that the leader and their followers can be blessed. The scriptures state in Malachi 3:10 "to bring ye all the tithes into the storehouse, that there may be meat in mine house, and prove me now herewith, saith the LORD of hosts, if I will not open you the windows of heaven, and pour you out a blessing, that there shall not be room enough to receive it." The church leader must be first partaker in showing its followers how to be biblically blessed. These are the basic principles of any mature believer and the church leader must possess this level of maturity if they desire to lead effectively.

2. They should never be distracted in their purpose and their kingdom assignment. Your purpose is the reason you were created and for many leaders this is an area of struggle. How can you lead a group of people but not know your purpose? So many leaders get distracted by trying to lead without first knowing who they are.

It's the leaders' job to know their purpose and the reason why they were created by first seeking God and mediating on his word. Also, leaders should never be distracted in their assignment, which is the task that God gave them to execute in the earth. If the leader is a preacher or minister, he or she should know how to minister or preach effectively to the assigned audience. If the leader is a deacon, he or she should know all of the duties that the deaconate entails and fulfill it. If the leader is a trustee, he or she should know about finances and how to govern the church financially. If the leader doesn't know the assignment, how can one successfully lead?

3. The leader should never be distracted in character and integrity. Character is who you are and your core values that cannot be compromised. Integrity is what you do with who you say you are.

One question: "Does what you do line up with who you say you are?" This can be one of the greatest distractions in leadership, when people cannot trust what you say; it becomes very difficult for them to follow you. As a leader, mean what you say and live up to it so that you won't break the trust between you and your followers.

Next let's take a look at the distraction of pride in church leadership. This distraction is prevalent in church leadership. The church leader must be very careful not to fall into this trap of deception that they have made it on their own because of what they have accomplished all by themselves. These statements must never be a part of the leader's vocabulary: "What I have been doing," "I have been doing this all by myself," "Nobody ever helped me," "I, I, I, Me, Me, Me, and this is how I feel!" Your pride and your feelings can be your greatest distraction. One thing that you must remember is that you are never alone and that you have the assistance and help of God always. You must remember that we are nothing without Him. We are mere servants of the most-high God. As leaders we have been commissioned by God to serve the people that follow us. Even Jesus Himself states in Mark 10:45, "For even He the Son of Man did not come to be served, but to serve, and to give his life as a ransom for many." The servant leaders must learn to give up their lives and their desires for the greater good of those they are leading.

Lastly, let's take a look at the distraction of unproductive busyness: Busy and stuck in the same routine day after day with no RESULTS. Doing ten things and not accomplishing one thing. This distraction has cost many leaders vital time. Have you ever considered accomplishing one objective or task at a time? Some leaders take on too many tasks at one time, which cause us not to accomplish anything at all. We must learn as leaders not to be distracted by unproductive busyness, stuck doing the same stuff Sunday after Sunday, week after week with nothing to show for it. I dare you to focus on the one thing and to execute it, fulfill it and check it off your list so that you can move on to the next task.

This has allowed many of us to arrive at our destinations too late. Beloved, there is a difference between arriving at a place on time and arriving at a place too late. If there is an event scheduled in Washington, DC that begins at 1pm and ends at 5pm on a Saturday evening and you and your followers arrive at 6pm, you and your followers have made it to the destination but have arrived too late. Timing is everything; you can arrive at the right place at the wrong time. Maybe it was the traffic or something in our homes that distracted us from arriving on time, but as leaders we must be mindful of the potential distractions that we may encounter on our road to destiny. We must learn as leaders to start early and to forecast and anticipate the distractions that may prevent us from arriving on time.

You must become a leader that's focused so that you can be effective and your followers can go to that place that only you can take them with the help of our Lord and Savior Jesus Christ.

Chapter V

Fatal Distractions

Chapter V
Fatal Distractions

Fatal distractions are similar to fatal attractions. A fatal attraction occurs when a person becomes so morbidly infatuated with a person that the infatuation becomes dangerous. A person will then go to any extent until he or she get what they desire. A fatal attraction is one that doesn't end well for the perpetrator because at the end of the day many times the infatuation doesn't get fulfilled. On the other hand, a fatal distraction occurs when someone becomes so infatuated with a person or thing that the infatuation fatally draws his or her attention away from what's important and vital and it eventually ends in either a spiritual or physical death.

This chapter on fatal distractions has been written out of sheer experience. I must testify that there was an instance in my life where I had become a victim of someone who had a fatal attraction towards me. This young lady confessed her desires to me and the moment that I said that I didn't share those same desires, the friendship turned ugly. Because of her infatuation, her behavior resorted to stalking and harassment.

This behavior left me feeling uneasy at the thought of an individual that was determined that she wouldn't stop until she fulfilled what she desired with me. Her persistence was one that I had never experienced before. I often found myself rehearsing in my head what this person could potentially do to me, to the point where I began to allow it to distract me. It was at this point, that I realized that the spirit of distraction was real. After long thought, prayer, and wise counsel, I had to obtain a peace order against this person. It took time, money, and energy away from what I should have been doing, including writing this book. I found myself sitting in a court room, waiting to go before the judge amidst individuals that were extremely distracted. This person was sent to destroy my character, and she was extremely determined not to give up until she was successful.

As I sat in the courtroom it dawned on me that distractions can be fatal. It confirmed to me that this situation definitely was a distraction sent straight from the pit of hell. That the spirit of distraction is real and it comes to suck the life right out of you. I often prayed, "Lord why me?" And His answer was, "Why not you? FEAR NOT! I AM with you, Greg! You thought you would write a book on distractions and that you would not experience them for yourself." Wow! I had to be the first partaker and actually live it. It wasn't an easy task to stand in court and look my distraction dead in the face and stay calm. I really wanted to tell her how I really felt however, with the help of God I didn't give in to the distraction. I can remember each time that I wanted to respond to defend myself, the judge declared: "Mr. Johnson, keep quiet." I finally realized that some things are not worth responding to and that I needed to forgive her in spite of the situation.

You must understand, beloved that the devil will go to any extent to make sure that you don't arrive at your destination at the appointed time. But you must stand confident on the fact that our God will go to any extent, I mean any extent, to protect, preserve and keep those who are His. There are so many people who are fatally distracted and they don't even know it. They can't see danger and they can't see the end result of their distractions. However, you who are reading this book will know and be able to recognize those fatal distractions when they present themselves in your lives.

Sometimes we can be so focused on the distraction that we never recognize the bigger picture and the greater assignment of the distraction, which is to get you off course, off focus, and to delay your assignment. It was the job of the devil to get me to focus on the situation and what could potentially happen. With hopes that he would delay some of the goals and assignments that the Lord had set before me, his ultimate goal was that it would end as a fatality. However, this tactic didn't work, because I remained focused. Beloved!! The distractions in your life have the potential to become fatal if not confronted. But with Jesus as your protector, you know that a thousand can fall at thy side and ten thousand at thy right hand. It shall not come near your dwelling.

I'm reminded in scripture of the story of Samson and Delilah in Judges Chapter 16, where a woman named Delilah in the valley of Sorek through much persistence and nagging got Samson to reveal the secret to his strength. Finally in verse 17 of that same chapter, Samson reveals his weakness to (his distraction) Delilah. Samson was so distracted by the persistence of Delilah that he gave the enemy the secret to his strength. He was so distracted that he couldn't see that he was putting himself in danger and in harm's way. He couldn't see the fatality of the situation until his strength was gone and his eyes were gouged out. Unfortunately my brother or my sister, you can be so distracted that you won't even see the fatal blow of the enemy coming your way. You can be so deeply distracted that you lose sight of your very purpose and it may even cost you your life.

I'm reminded of a high profile murder case here in Baltimore, where an innocent young man was murdered on the bus stop moments after he left his job. He was a great and respectable young man, a young man who had committed his life to saving the lives of others, particularly those who had fallen victim to senseless acts of violence, only to find himself a victim of that same violence that he had helped countless others through so many times. He found himself in the dead center of a vicious gang war that had arisen on the very bus stop where he was standing. He was standing amidst danger and he couldn't see it and in turn he was used as a human shield.

The family contacted me to preach the eulogy at his funeral. Automatically, my compassion went out to the family and suddenly in the midst of the conversation it hit me like a ton of bricks. One of the family members said, "Greg, he didn't even see it coming because he had his earphones in." This statement just added to my devastation because I said to myself, "Greg!! If only he was alert and conscious of his surrounding, he may have sensed that danger was near." He was standing in the midst of a danger zone and had absolutely no idea that it would cost him his life. I'm sure that if he had recognized some early warning signs he may have run for cover.

Today, I honor the life of this young man because it's through this situation that I had an opportunity to look through the pain, devastation, and hurt of the moment and receive one of the greatest lessons that could potentially save the lives of others. That lesson is "No More Distractions!!!" Focus on your surroundings and pay close attention to where you are. It may just save your life. God speaks through signs and gut feelings. I honor this young man's life because he wasn't in the wrong place at the wrong time. He was just surrounded by some young men that had allowed their lives to be fatally distracted and they in turn took the life of an innocent young man who was just a bystander.

I'm also reminded of another story that saddened me; it's the story of a young lady who allowed the distractions of this life to torment her to the point where she took her life. She made a permanent decision on some temporary distractions that if recognized and dealt with, could have been eliminated and she could still be living today. She allowed the enemy to speak to her and she believed every single lie that he told her. I write to minister to you and to declare to you: "Don't buy into the LIE!" It's a distraction.

I've encountered so many that were depressed and are tormented by the spirit of suicide. They have allowed the spirit of suicide to distract them from wanting to live. Because of the trials, issues, and pains of this life, they have allowed the thief to distract them from living abundantly. The Bible states in John 10:10 that, "the thief comes to steal, kill and destroy." I must stop at that word DESTROY which means to wipe you off of the face of the earth as if you never existed. However, I thank & praise God at the "But" in the text that states, "...but He [Jesus] came that we might have life and that they may have it more abundantly." I dare you, if your life has been affected or is being tormented by the spirit of suicide, to declare the word of God over your life. You must open your mouth and declare Psalm 118:17 which states, "I will not die but live, and will proclaim what the Lord has done." You must declare Philippians 4:13, which states, "that you can do all things through Christ Jesus which strengthens you." I want you to know that you are not alone, I'm conscious of the fact that the devil wants to isolate you, but the book of Isaiah chapter 41 verse 10 states, "Fear not, for I am with you; be not dismayed, for I am your God; I will strengthen you, I will help you, I will uphold you with My righteous right hand." You must be confident, beloved, that you are not in this by yourself. You have the help of our Lord with you. This heaviness is yet a distraction and today it must leave. The word of God says in Isaiah 61:3 to "put on the garment of praise instead of a faint spirit, a spirit of mourning, despair, or heaviness that you may be like an oak tree planted by the Lord to reveal His splendor." The distraction of suicide must be no more.

We see in the book of Genesis a familiar story that has been taught to us at a young age either in Sunday school or by just listening to our parents; explain a story of where we come from. That story is the story of Adam and Eve. We see in Genesis 2:16-17 that God gave a commandment to Adam: "Of every tree of the garden thou may freely eat: But of the tree of the knowledge of good and evil, thou shalt not eat of it: for in the day that thou eat thereof thou shalt surely die." By chapter 3, a distraction appears in the form of a serpent whose objective is to make Adam and Eve go against the commandment and the will of God for their lives.

The Bible says that the serpent was more subtle than any beast of the field and because Eve gave a listening ear to him she became fatally distracted and eventually believed the LIE. She knew the commandment because she repeated it back to the serpent. She declares it in verse 3: "But of the fruit of the tree which is in the midst of the garden, God said, ye shall not eat of it, neither shall ye touch it, lest ye die." The serpent responds in verses 4 and 5: "Ye shall not surely die: For God knows that in the day ye eat thereof, then your eyes shall open and you shall be as gods [with the little g], knowing good and evil." The serpent succeeded by distracting Eve from her purpose, which was to be a help-meet to her husband Adam. The tree looked good and was pleasing to the eye, especially at the thought of being wise or god-like, she went against the commandment of God, touched the fruit, ate the fruit, and gave some to her husband who ate it too. They knew the commandment and they knew the consequences of their disobedience. But because they were so distracted by the lie of the serpent and how good it looked and how much wiser it would make them, they couldn't even see the part in the commandment where God said "You shall surely die."

I come to tell you, my brother or my sister, that the life that Adam and Eve lived before the fatal distraction was so much better. They had everything they needed, they worked in complete harmony with God and now here it is because their focus has now been distorted and their attention has now been drawn away from God. They are ashamed to be in His presence. The distractions come into our lives to draw us away from God and His plan for our lives. If we are not careful, we will find ourselves on the outside of the garden (outside of His will and outside of His presence), driven out and taken away by our own disobedience because we were distracted. Because Eve was distracted by the serpent and Adam was distracted by the moment and did not stand up for what was right. It wasn't until Adam ate from the tree that their eyes were opened, their innocence was taken and the knowledge of evil was present. It was God who gave Adam the original commandment so that he had to take full responsibility. Unfortunately, the end result thereof was fatal because their oldest son murdered their youngest son. How devastating this must have been! This is the first human death recorded in the scriptures and unfortunately they couldn't see this while they were entertaining the distraction, because they were so distracted by the beauty and how pleasing the tree looked.

Beloved, distractions are real and many times we never look at them as being fatal. I have seen countless times in the media where individuals were so distracted by texting and driving or talking on their cell phones while driving, that they ended up killing themselves and also killing innocent people. The end is always tragic and at the dead center of it all was a great big distraction. Beloved, at this very moment as I am writing this book, I'm pleading with you to recognize and eliminate any of the distractions in your life that have the potential to end as a fatality. Believe me, that distraction is not worth dying for, whether it's spiritual or physical. "IT'S NOT WORTH IT!"

"The wealthiest places in the world are not gold mines, oil fields, diamond mines or banks. The wealthiest place is the cemetery. There lies companies that were never started, masterpieces that were never painted... In the cemetery there is buried the greatest treasure of untapped potential. There is a treasure within you that must come out. Don't go to the grave with your treasure still within YOU." – Dr. Myles Munroe.

Because of the distractions of our lives I have seen countless lives cut down prematurely before individuals made their impact, dent, and impartation into the earth. They left this world with untapped potential as Dr. Munroe states above, having not released the treasure that they were born with because somewhere on this road and journey called life, they became fatally distracted. But today is your day to put away the distractions and live. Live, my brother, Live, my sister, LIVE!!! There is life all around you! It's your time to LIVE!

Chapter VI

Recognizing Your Distractions

Chapter VI

Recognizing Your Distractions

It was Beverly R. Ames who warned to "beware when distractions come your way. That you'll know that it's a distraction when you stop doing what you're supposed to be doing and find yourself pondering things that have no value."

The first step to living an undistracted life is to first recognize your distractions. If you are going to be headed to a place of being undistracted you must first admit that there are distractions in your life. Out of all of the chapters in this book, this chapter is very important because it's about you making an important decision that will affect the rest of your life. You have come to a crossroad of making a choice and that choice is whether you desire to be undistracted or distracted?

Now that you have made it to this chapter you should have a clear idea whether you are distracted or undistracted. Now is the time for you to dig deep down within yourself, your mind, and your experiences, and begin to confront and recognize every one of the distractions that have kept you from moving forward and enjoying your life. This will be a journey of real soul searching and transformation. However, this journey will require you to visit places and experiences, maybe even people you don't actually want to revisit. But it's imperative that you make a decision with the guidance of the Holy Spirit so that you can begin to live again. Distractions are the enemy of focus and the enemy of each of our destinies. Their objective is to get us to waste valuable time on frivolous things that don't matter so that we can forfeit our destiny or arrive late. You must obtain the attitude that "I refuse to allow anything to distract me from my destiny." Today is your day beloved, to expose the distractions in your life so that they can no longer function. There is a great task before you, and trust me, life is better when it's undistracted.

Let's visit some of life's most common distractions, and if you can identify with any of them I would like for you to include them on the distraction worksheet on pages 72 and 73 of this book. These are things, people, and situations that pull many of us away from our purpose, our assignment and our tasks. Let's confront your distractions.

LIST OF COMMON DISTRACTIONS:

The Distraction of:

❖ ABANDONMENT - deserted by the utterly forsaken.

❖ A PRESENT RELATIONSHIP - a relationship you are currently in.

❖ ADDICTION TO SEX - obsession with sex.

❖ ADULTERY - breaking of covenant.

❖ AN EX-RELATIONSHIP - holding on to a past relationship.

❖ ANXIETY - uneasiness of mind.

❖ ARROGANCE - an attitude of being better than another.

❖ ASSUMPTIONS - a thing that is accepted as true or as certain to happen, without proof.

❖ BEING AN OVER ACHIEVER - obsession with achieving.

❖ BEING UNBALANCED - having no balance.

❖ BEING AN UNDER ACHIEVER - doing the bare minimum.

❖ BIRTH DEFECTS - imperfections that you were born with.

❖ BITTERNESS - a deep-seated ill will.

❖ BLAMING OTHERS - placing the fault on others.

❖ BURDENS OF OTHERS - taking on problems of others.

❖ CELL PHONE - ringing, messaging, calls, and over use.

- ❖ CHAOS - complete disorder and confusion.

- ❖ CHASING MONEY - money as your main focus.

- ❖ CONFUSION - lack of understanding; uncertainty.

- ❖ CONTROL - prevent from flourishing to hold back.

- ❖ COVETOUSNESS - wrong desires of wealth or possessions.

- ❖ DAY DREAMING - detachment from one's surroundings.

- ❖ DEATH OF A LOVED ONE - loss of a close relative.

- ❖ DEBT - money owed by one party.

- ❖ DECEPTION - making someone believe something that is not true.

- ❖ DENIAL - refusing to believe what is real.

- ❖ DEPRESSION - depressing your feelings and emotions.

- ❖ DISAPPOINTMENTS - the feeling of sadness or displeasure caused by the un-fulfillment of one's hopes or expectations.

- ❖ DISAPPROVAL - how others stress their disapproval of you.

- ❖ DISCONTENTMENT - being dissatisfied.

- ❖ DISCOURAGEMENT - feeling of having lost hope or confidence.

- ❖ DISOBEDIENCE - not being obedient.

- ❖ DISORDER - chaos and not being organized.

- ❖ DISTRACTING RELATIONSHIPS - relationships that pull you away.

- ❖ DISTRUST - the lack of trust.

- ❖ DOUBT - hesitant to believe.

- ❖ EMAIL OBSESSION SYNDROME - checking your emails excessively.

- ❖ EMOTIONS - how you feel.

- ❖ ENTITLEMENT - claiming rights and ownership.

- ❖ ENVY - a feeling of resentment aroused by someone else's possessions or qualities.

- ❖ EXCUSES - poor or inadequate reasons to not accomplish a task.

- ❖ FACEBOOK & SOCIAL MEDIA - constant viewing.

- ❖ FAILURE - the omission of an expected or required action.

- ❖ FALSE HOPES & EXPECTATIONS - the desire to obtain unrealistic outcomes.

- ❖ FEAR - being afraid of the outcome or what's next.

- ❖ FEELINGS OF BEING UNWANTED - not good enough.

- ❖ FEELINGS OF INADEQUACY - not having what it takes.

- ❖ FEELINGS OF LONELINESS - feelings of being by yourself.

- ❖ FEELINGS OF NOT BEING LOVED - you aren't loved.

- ❖ FOOD - The love of food to the point it affects your health.

- ❖ FUTURE EVENTS - worried about what's happening next.

- ❖ GAMBLING - taking chances.

- ❖ GREED - the selfish and excessive desire for more of something than is needed.

- ❖ GRIEVING - multifaceted response to a loss.

- ❖ HATE - intense or passionate dislike.

- ❖ HEARTBREAK - pain from someone who broke your heart.

- ❖ HOLDING GRUDGES - not letting go.

- ❖ ILL-SPOKEN WORDS - harsh words towards a person.

- ❖ IMPAIRED AND DISTORTED JUDGMENT - bad decisions.

- ❖ IMPATIENCE - inability to wait.

- ❖ INSECURITIES - lack of confidence.

- ❖ INSTANT GRATIFICATION - immediate satisfaction.

- ❖ JEALOUSY - resentment against another's success.

- ❖ LACK OF FAITH - doubt and faint in your faith.

- ❖ LAZINESS - slow moving and sluggish.

- ❖ LOOKING FOR LOVE - searching for love in all the wrong places.

- ❖ LOW SELF-ESTEEM - low evaluation of one's worth.

- ❖ LUST - very strong sexual desire.

- ❖ LYING - not telling the truth.

- ❖ MATERIAL POSSESSIONS - things of this world.

- ❖ MENTAL ABUSE - psychological trauma.

- ❖ MOLESTATION - improperly touched in a sexual way.

- ❖ NEGATIVE INFLUENCE - negative people and situations.

- ❖ NERVOUSNESS - unnaturally or acutely uneasy or apprehensive.

- ❖ NO VISION - no view of your purpose.

- ❖ OBSESSIVE BEHAVIORS - uneasiness, apprehension, fear or worry.

- ❖ OTHERS' PERECEPTION - how others view you.

- ❖ OURSELVES - self getting in the way of purpose.

- ❖ OVER EATING - eating after you are full.

- ❖ OVER THINKING - thinking too much into it.

- ❖ OVER WORKED - worked with no appreciation.

- ❖ PARANOIA - a thought process influenced by anxiety.

- ❖ PAST HURTS - deep hurt from 10 and 15 years ago.

- ❖ PEER PRESSURE - behaviors to conform to a group's norms.

- ❖ PERFECTION - the act of pretending to be free from flaws.

- ❖ PHOBIAS – excessive fear of an object or situation.

- ❖ PHYSICAL ABUSE - physical pain, injury, or bodily harm.

- ❖ PLEASING MAN - to do any or everything to please man.

- ❖ POOR MULTI-TASKING - poorly doing too many things at one time.

- ❖ POOR QUALITY OF LIFE - your living conditions.

- ❖ PORNOGRAPHY - portrayal of sexual subject matter.

- ❖ PRE-MARITAL SEX - sex when not married.

- ❖ PREJUDICE - make biased and cast judgment.

- ❖ PRIDE - inflated sense of one's personal status.

- ❖ PROCRASTINATION - putting off or delaying.

- ❖ RAPE - sexual abuse and unlawful sexual contact.

- ❖ REBELLIOUS CHILDREN - wayward children.

- ❖ REJECTION - being turned away by people you admire or want to be a part of.

- ❖ RELATIONSHIPS - the people that you are in constant communication and fellowship with.

- ❖ RESENTMENT - bitter at having been treated unfairly.

- ❖ SELF-GAIN - what you can get out of it.

- ❖ SELF PERCEPTION - how you see yourself.

- ❖ SELF PITY - feeling sorry for one's self.

- ❖ SELF-RIGHTEOUSNESS - holier than thou attitudes.

- ❖ SERVING THE CHURCH - serving without relationship.

- ❖ SICKNESS - afflictions, sickness and diseases.

- ❖ SKIN COLOR - how you feel about the pigment of your skin.

- ❖ STEREOTYPES - a fixed view of a person or thing.

- ❖ SUBSTANCE ABUSE - abusing drugs, alcohol.

- ❖ SUICIDE - ending one's life.

- ❖ SUPERFICIAL LOVE - love without substance.

- ❖ TELEVISION - watching excessive television shows.

- ❖ TEMPTATION - a desire to do something, especially something wrong or unwise.

- ❖ TEXTURE OF YOUR HAIR - not liking the texture of your hair.

- ❖ THE AMERICAN DREAM - perfect life without troubles.

- ❖ THE FEAR OF DYING - anxiety about dying.

- ❖ THE INTERNET - distracted by the World Wide Web.

- ❖ THE MEDIA - the influences of the media in all areas.

- ❖ THE OUTCOME OF A SITUATION - what could happen?

- ❖ THINGS THAT YOU CAN'T CHANGE - the unchangeable.

- ❖ TIREDNESS - feelings of fatigue.

- ❖ TOO MUCH RESPONSIBILITY - feeling overwhelmed.

- ❖ UNCOMPASSIONATE - not showing compassion.

- ❖ UNFORGIVENESS - not releasing or letting go.

- ❖ UNFULFILLMENT - failure to fulfill.

- ❖ UNPRODUCTIVE BUSYNESS - nothing is accomplished.

- ❖ UNRESOLVED ISSUES - issues that haven't been handled.

- ❖ UNWORTHINESS – ones lack of value, undeserving.

- ❖ VERBAL ABUSE - negative statements towards a person.

- ❖ WEIGHT - weighing too much or too little.

- ❖ WORRY - dwelling on difficulties or troubles.

MY LIST OF DISTRACTIONS

REFOCUS, READJUST & RESTART!

NO MORE DISTRACTIONS

MY LIST OF DISTRACTIONS

REFOCUS, READJUST & RESTART!

NO MORE
DISTRACTIONS

WWW.GREGOJOHNSON.NET

Chapter VII

Dating Your Distraction

Chapter VII
Dating Your Distraction

Let's begin this chapter with a question. Have you ever dated someone or are currently dating someone who has distracted you from your goals, dreams, and aspirations? If you have answered yes to any of these questions, this chapter was inspired just for you. This chapter on "Dating Your Distraction" I believe, is my second favorite chapter in the entire book, because I have had the opportunity to discuss this chapter with a couple of my single and married friends who have given me a lot of positive and helpful input on this subject. I first would like to thank each of them for helping with this chapter. Ok, let's begin.

Many of us, single or married, can attest to the fact that we have had our fair share of dating people that were a complete waste of our time, energy, and resources. Ultimately they were a great big distraction. For you who are still dating your distraction, and for others of you who have even married their distraction, this chapter is a great chapter. Beloved, I have realized that if you entertain a distraction long enough it will eventually overtake and distract you. We must remember that we play an important role in actually how long we choose to date and entertain our distraction.

For some of us, it only took the first date, and we knew that person that we were dating was a distraction. However, there are others who have found themselves five, six, and twenty years into the relationship. Unfortunately, it's very difficult to leave a distraction when your feelings and emotions are involved, when there is a shared apartment or home, and even kids involved. So some have asked, "How do you walk away from all of that, when that's what you've been accustomed to?" Maybe, just maybe, the choice to stay doesn't solely rely on the distraction, but is based upon the benefits that you gain from the distraction's just being there. Or maybe you are staying simply because it seems to be the right choice at the moment.

I've learned that one of the reasons why we continue to date our distractions is because of what others might say or think about the relationship. Others stay because they have resolved within themselves that they have messed up their lives to the point that they think there is no one else out there who wants them. This is a complete lie and a ploy of the enemy to get them to stay in an unhealthy relationship that benefits neither party.

Let's first explore the warning signs that the relationship or the person that you are dating is a distraction. The first sign that they are a distraction is that they take from you and never replace or add to who you already are. They don't enhance who you are and instead there is this constant depletion of your time, energy, love, and resources without replenishment. Any relationship in your life should make you a better you. If there are constant withdrawals with no deposits you'll eventually be bankrupt. The relationship should add or increase value to you.

Another warning sign is stagnation or a steady decline of who you are. It's a place of being stuck or held back. Have you considered that from the very moment that you have met the person who distracts you, there has been a hold and stand still of your dreams, ambitions, and goals? Have you considered that this individual has totally made you give them your complete attention for the sake of losing focus of the goals and the focus that you had before you met them? This is the testimony of many singles and even married couples: they feel as if the person they are dating or married to is not bearing fruit or headed in the same direction that they are.

Another warning sign that you are dating your distraction is that you are in love with a potential person instead of the reality of who they are right now. Many times we enter into relationships with people with a hope that they will change and become the person that we desire. One of my destiny partners, Minister Shawnta Clark shared with me that, "We fall in love with the potential them and many times become victims of heartbreaks that have left us scarred and wounded and ultimately blinded and immune to real genuine love."

I have spoken with so many people and have asked what's making you stay with them and they in turn stress to me, "Greg, I believe that they'll change or I believe that I can change them." And they enter into false hopes and false realities because many times that person will never change. Therefore we waste months if not years of our time with a distraction that has left us worse off than we were before we met them. There is a famous quote that states that when a person shows you who they are, believe them. So if we encounter too many of these distractions on our dating journey, when the real person that God has ordained for us arrives in our lives it's difficult for us to recognize them. Or we turn them away or drive them away, by treating them as if they were the other distractions that we've dated. Because our hearts have been through so many traumas we reject real genuine agape love that is selfless, and unconditional, and has no limits or boundaries. We reject the creative love, a love that loves just because, and a love that is not superficial, a love that's demonstrated instead of just spoken to us. Because our last heartbreak and disappointment has distracted us from loving the one that God has sent our way. So we date distraction after distraction, and we can almost predict the outcome every time. And our question is, "When I will ever find the right one?"

Many of us have had our fair share of dating our distractions, which left us sometimes asking God, if our expectations are real, are our standards too high, or will we ever find the right person? However, I am convinced, after dating distraction after distraction that if we just wait and follow God's plan for dating and for our lives, He will send us the one whom he created for us, our rib, our help-meet.

We see throughout scripture those who were in relationships that distracted them. Relationships are covenants and must never be taken lightly.

Here are some of the warning signs that you are dating your distraction. The person that you are dating:

Doesn't believe the same things that you believe. The Bible says, how can two walk together except they agree.

When the relationship you're in is God ordained there will be harmony, there will be a connection, there will be a flow. The Bible states in Genesis 2:20 that "God put Adam into a deep sleep and made a woman for him. Which means God didn't need Adam's direct assistance in what he needed in companionship."

Adam had no say so in how she would look, how long her hair would be, what abilities she possessed. He had just awakened from a deep sleep and there she was. He didn't go searching to find her; God presented her to him at the perfect moment and opened his eyes. I often questioned in my mind the reason why God didn't request Adam's input in the making of Eve. So as I pondered, the first thing to come to my mind was that as humans we are first driven and stimulated by what we see. Even Adam reveals this notion in verse 23, when at first glimpse of Eve he describes her appearance, "this is now bone of my bones and flesh of my flesh." What Adam saw at first sight was his mirrored image in the woman that was created for him without his long list of requirements and 'must haves.' I can just imagine what his first sight of her was like, I imagine that he examined her and looked at her very closely and he may have even looked deeper and found out that this is my helper. Many times we date and enter into relationships with people who don't mirror us and when we look at them we don't see ourselves, and in turn we get so caught up on their external looks and our personal preferences that we allow those preferences to distract us from the person, leaving us heartbroken and disappointed because they were not who we perceived them to be.

I've learned that everything with a good outer appearance may not be good for me. In the words of my mother, "Everything that glitters is not gold." You must remember that some of the greatest distractions come wrapped up in long hair, a pretty face, a nice shape, a perfectly toned body, a handsome face, and a convincing grin. Once, unwrapped they can be revealed to be one of the greatest distractions that you have ever encountered. You must make up in your mind today that you are no longer going to be distracted by what they look like. I dare you to begin to unwrap them and see what's behind all of that makeup and that perfectly toned body and see the real person. You've been blinded by looks long enough, because at the end of the day looks are not enough. You need more than just looks, you need a person that God has made just for you, a person that has the spirit of God, morals, character, integrity, respect, commitment, accountability, responsibility, unconditional love, a future, a genuine connection, and selflessness. You need someone that will push you to be a better you. You need a motivator, one that has the capabilities to help you manifest your dreams and one that will pray for you and help you complete your purpose on the earth. Beloved, they can only come to you by the leading of God. But if you are so used to dating your distraction, will you recognize them when they appear?

Another sign that we're dating our distraction is jealousy of our success of progress. We must be very careful of this trait in the person that we are dating. Jealousy is resentment against a person enjoying success or advantage. Have you ever dated someone who tried to talk you out of your dreams and goals? Have you dated someone who makes it their business to belittle you and tell you all the things that you are not? Have you dated someone who points out all of your flaws? If your response to any of those questions was "Yes!" guess what, you are dating your distraction. It's time for you to wake up and smell the coffee. You deserve so much better. My mother used to say that, "I can do bad all by myself." It's time to stop allowing that jealous distraction to hinder you. They have eaten away too much of your time already. I dare you to make a decision today, to walk right away from your distraction.

Chapter VIII

Eliminating Your Distraction

Chapter VIII

Eliminating Your Distraction

Once you have recognized your distractions, you can now begin to eliminate them. Please visit the list of distractions that you have identified. Let's begin the process to eliminate them using the word of God.

First let us pray:

Father, in the precious name of Jesus, I thank you for my brother or my sister. I ask today that you enter into the place where they are residing. I ask that you allow them to feel the warmth of your embrace as an indication that you are with them. Let them know that they are never alone, no matter where they are. Father, I pray to you today concerning the journey that you have them on of eliminating their distractions. Their distractions have held them up long enough and have robbed them of their time, resources and energy. Today I ask that you rid them of any distractions that have gotten in their way. I declare that every distraction will scatter in the name of Jesus. I call out the spirit of distraction that has come to kill time and waste their time. I declare that the spirit of focus and productivity will enter into their lives right now in the name of Jesus. Amen

My brother or my sister, I'm quite sure that there are many distractions that you have recognized and listed on your list of distractions from chapter six. Having recognized them, you have begun your journey of eliminating them, which I must admit may not be an easy task for you, especially if the distraction has had your attention for a long time. The long list of distractions, which I have compiled with the help and assistance of a few friends, is just a drop in the bucket compared to the many other distractions that we haven't pointed out.

I've learned that sometimes helping others that are distracted can distract you. Have you ever tried helping someone from the goodness and kindness of your heart and they eventually abused and mistreated you? Have you ever been a victim of a family member and friend whom you have tried to help and later they stabbed you in your back or hurt you? Have you ever suffered for the sake of helping someone else who later didn't appreciate your sacrifice? If you have answered yes to any of these questions it's time to begin eliminating your distractions.

We must remember that the distractions in their lives have the potential to spill over into ours if they aren't eliminated.

It's time to eliminate these distractions by using:

The word of God.

WE ELIMINATE THE DISTRACTION OF

❖ ABANDONMENT - *Joshua 1:9* - "Have I not commanded you? Be strong and courageous. Do not be frightened, and do not be dismayed, for the Lord your God is with you wherever you go."

❖ A PRESENT RELATIONSHIP - *Proverbs 13:20* - "Keep Company with the wise and you will become wise. If you make friends with stupid people, you will be ruined."

❖ ADDICTION TO SEX - *Titus 2:11-14* - "For the grace of God that bringeth salvation hath appeared to all men, Teaching us that, denying ungodliness and worldly lusts, we should live soberly, righteously, and godly, in this present world; Looking for that blessed hope, and the glorious appearing of the great God and our Saviour Jesus Christ; Who gave himself for us, that he might redeem us from all iniquity, and purify unto himself a peculiar people, zealous of good works."

❖ ADULTERY - *II Corinthians 6:18* - "Flee fornication. Every sin that a man doeth is without the body; but he that committeth fornication sinneth against his own body."

❖ AN EX-RELATIONSHIP - *Isaiah 43:18* - "Forget the former things; do not dwell on the past."

❖ ANXIETY - *Philippians 4:6* - "Do not be anxious about anything, but in every situation, by prayer and petition, with thanksgiving, present your requests to God."

❖ ARROGANCE - *I Samuel 2:3* - "Talk no more so very proudly, let not arrogance come from your mouth; for the Lord is a God of knowledge, and by him actions are weighed."

❖ ASSUMPTIONS - *Proverbs 18:2* - "A fool takes no pleasure in understanding, but only in expressing his opinion."

❖ BEING AN OVER ACHIEVER - *II Timothy 3:17* - "That the man of God may be competent, equipped for every good work."

❖ BEING UNBALANCED - *Ecclesiastes 7:16* - "Do not be excessively righteous and do not be overly wise. Why should you ruin yourself?"

❖ BEING AN UNDER ACHIEVER - *Philippians 4:13* - "I can do all things through him who strengthens me."

❖ BIRTH DEFECTS - *Psalm 139:14* - "I will praise thee; for I am fearfully and wonderfully made: marvelous are thy works; and that my soul knoweth right well."

❖ BITTERNESS - *Ephesians 4:31* - "Get rid of all bitterness, rage and anger, brawling and slander, along with every form of malice."

❖ BLAMING OTHERS - *Jude 1:16-20* - "These people are always grumbling and blaming others; they follow their own evil desires; they brag about themselves and flatter others in order to get their own way. But remember, my friends, what you were told in the past by the apostles of our Lord Jesus Christ. They said to you, "When the last days come, people will appear who will make fun of you, people who follow their own godless desires." These are the people who cause divisions, who are controlled by their natural desires, who do not have the Spirit. But you, my friends, keep on building yourselves up on your most sacred faith. Pray in the power of the Holy Spirit."

❖ BURDENS OF OTHERS - *Galatians 6:2* - "Bear ye one another's burdens, and so fulfill the law of Christ."

❖ CELL PHONE - *Proverbs 4:25-27* - "Keep looking straight ahead, without turning aside. Know where you are headed, and you will stay on solid ground. Don't make a mistake by turning to the right or the left."

❖ CHAOS - *II Corinthians 14:33* - "For God is not a God of disorder but of peace--as in all the congregations of the Lord's people."

❖ CHASING MONEY - *II Timothy 6:10* - "For the love of money is a root of all kinds of evils. It is through this craving that some have wandered away from the faith and pierced themselves with many pangs."

❖ CONFUSION - *I Corinthians 14:33* - "For God is not a God of confusion but of peace."

❖ CONTROL - *Galatians 5:1* - "Stand fast in the liberty wherewith Christ hath made us free, and not allow ourselves to again be entangled in the yoke of bondage."

❖ COVETOUSNESS - *Luke 12:15* - "And he said unto them, Take heed, and beware of covetousness: for a man's life consisteth not in the abundance of the things which he possesseth."

❖ DAY DREAMING - *Ecclesiastes 5:3* - "Daydreaming comes when there are too many worries. Careless speaking comes when there are too many words."

❖ DEATH OF A LOVED ONE - *I Thessalonians 4:13-17* - "But we do not want you to be uninformed, brothers, about those who are asleep, that you may not grieve as others do who have no hope. For since we believe that Jesus died and rose again, even so, through Jesus, God will bring with him those who have fallen asleep. For this we declare to you by a word from the Lord, that we who are alive, who are left until the coming of the Lord, will not precede those who have fallen asleep. For the Lord himself will descend from heaven with a cry of command, with the voice of an archangel, and with the sound of the trumpet of God. And the dead in Christ will rise first. Then we who are alive, who are left, will be caught up together with them in the clouds to meet the Lord in the air, and so we will always be with the Lord."

❖ DEBT - *Romans 13:7-8* - "Pay to all what is owed to them: taxes to whom taxes are owed, revenue to whom revenue is owed, respect to whom respect is owed, honor to whom honor is owed. Owe no one anything, except to love each other, for the one who loves another has fulfilled the law."

❖ DECEPTION - *Galatians 6:7-8* - "Be not deceived; God is not mocked: for whatsoever a man soweth, that shall he also reap. For he that soweth to his flesh shall of the flesh reap corruption; but he that soweth to the Spirit shall of the Spirit reap life everlasting."

- ❖ DENIAL - *I Corinthians 2:14* - "The natural person does not accept the things of the Spirit of God, for they are folly to him, and he is not able to understand them because they are spiritually discerned."

- ❖ DEPRESSION - *Matthew 11:28-30* - "Come to me, all who labor and are heavy laden, and I will give you rest. Take my yoke upon you, and learn from me, for I am gentle and lowly in heart, and you will find rest for your souls. For my yoke is easy, and my burden is light."

- ❖ DISAPPOINTMENTS - *Philippians 4:6-7* - "Be careful for nothing; but in everything by prayer and supplication with thanksgiving let your requests be made known unto God. And the peace of God, which passeth all understanding, shall keep your hearts and minds through Christ Jesus."

- ❖ DISAPPROVAL - *Hebrews 4:15* - "For we do not have a High Priest Who is unable to understand and sympathize and have a shared feeling with our weaknesses and infirmities and liability to the assaults of temptation, but One Who has been tempted in every respect as we are, yet without sinning."

- ❖ DISCONTENTMENT - *Hebrews 13:4* - "Keep your life free from love of money, and be content with what you have, for he has said, 'I will never leave you nor forsake you.'"

- ❖ DISCOURAGEMENT - *Jeremiah 29:11* - "For I know the plans I have for you, declares the Lord, plans for welfare and not for evil, to give you a future and a hope."

- ❖ DISOBEDIENCE - *John 14:15* - "If you love me, you will keep my commandments."

❖ DISORDER - *James 3:16* - "For where jealousy and selfish ambition exist, there will be disorder and every vile practice."

❖ DISTRACTING RELATIONSHIPS - *II Corinthians 6:14* - "Be ye not unequally yoked together with unbelievers: for what fellowship hath righteousness with unrighteousness? And what communion hath light with darkness?"

❖ DISTRUST - *Psalm 78:7* - "That they should put their confidence in God And not forget the works of God, But keep His commandments."

❖ DOUBT - *Proverbs 3:5-8* - "Trust in the Lord with all your heart, and do not lean on your own understanding. In all your ways acknowledge him, and he will make straight your paths. Be not wise in your own eyes; fear the Lord, and turn away from evil. It will be healing to your flesh and refreshment to your bones."

❖ EMAIL OBSESSION SYNDROME - *Matthew 6:34* - "Give your entire attention to what God is doing right now, and don't get worked up about what may or may not happen tomorrow. God will help you deal with whatever hard things come up when the time comes."

❖ EMOTIONS - *Proverbs 29:11* - "A fool gives full vent to his spirit but a wise man quietly holds it back."

❖ ENTITLEMENT - *II Thessalonians 3:10* - "While we were with you, we used to tell you, "Whoever refuses to work is not allowed to eat."

❖ ENVY - *James 3:16* - "For where envying and strife *is*, there *is* confusion and every evil work."

❖ EXCUSES - *Proverbs 26:13-16* - "The lazy person is full of excuses, saying, "I can't go outside because there might be a lion on the road! Yes, I'm sure there's a lion out there!" As a door turns back and forth on its hinges, so the lazy person turns over in bed. Some people are so lazy that they won't lift a finger to feed themselves. Lazy people consider themselves smarter than seven wise counselors."

❖ FACEBOOK & SOCIAL MEDIA - *Exodus 20:3-4* - "You shall have no other gods before me. You shall not make for yourself an idol in the form of anything in heaven above or on the earth beneath or in the waters below."

❖ FAILURE - *Philippians 4:13* - "I can do all things through Christ who strengthens me."

❖ FALSE HOPES & EXPECTATIONS - *Ephesians 5:6* - "Let no one deceive you with empty words, for because of these things the wrath of God comes upon the sons of disobedience."

❖ FEAR - *I Timothy 1:7* - "For God hath not given us the spirit of fear; but of power, and of love, and of a sound mind."

❖ FEELINGS OF BEING UNWANTED - *II Timothy 4: 16-17* - "At my first defense no one stood with me, but all forsook me. May it not be charged against them. But the Lord stood with me and strengthened me, so that the message might be preached fully through me, and that all the Gentiles might hear. Also I was delivered out of the mouth of the lion."

❖ FEELINGS OF INADEQUACY - *Ephesians 2:10* - "For we are His workmanship, created in Christ Jesus for good works, which God prepared beforehand so that we would walk in them."

❖ FEELINGS OF LONELINESS - *Isaiah 41:10* - "Fear not, for I am with you; be not dismayed, for I am your God; I will strengthen you, I will help you, I will uphold you with my righteous right hand."

❖ FEELINGS OF NOT BEING LOVED - *John 3:16* - "For God so loved the world, that he gave his only Son, that whoever believes in him should not perish but have eternal life."

❖ FOOD - *Colossians 3:2* - "Set your minds on things that are above, not on things that are on earth."

❖ FUTURE EVENTS - *Matthew 6:34* - "Therefore do not worry about tomorrow, for tomorrow will worry about itself. Each day has enough trouble of its own."

❖ GAMBLING - *Proverbs 13:11* - "Wealth gotten by vanity shall be diminished: but he that gathereth by labour shall increase."

❖ GREED - *Proverbs 28:25* - "A greedy man stirs up strife, but the one who trusts in the Lord will be enriched."

❖ GRIEVING - *Isaiah 41:10* - "So do not fear, for I am with you; do not be dismayed, for I am your God. I will strengthen you and help you; I will uphold you with my righteous right hand."

❖ HATE - *1 John 4:20* - "If anyone says, "I love God," and hates his brother, he is a liar; for he who does not love his brother whom he has seen cannot love God whom he has not seen."

❖ HEART BREAK - *Psalm 34:17-20* -" When the righteous cry for help, the Lord hears and delivers them out of all their troubles. The Lord is near to the brokenhearted and saves the crushed in spirit. Many are the afflictions of the righteous, but the Lord delivers him out of them all. He keeps all his bones; not one of them is broken."

❖ HOLDING GRUDGES - *Matthew 6:14-15* - "For if ye forgive men their trespasses, your heavenly Father will also forgive you: But if ye forgive not men their trespasses, neither will your Father forgive your trespasses."

❖ ILL-SPOKEN WORDS - *Ecclesiastes 7:21* - "Also take no heed unto all words that are spoken; lest thou hear thy servant curse thee:"

❖ IMPAIRED AND DISTORTED JUDGMENT - *Proverbs 14:12* - "There is a way that seems right to a man, but its end is the way to death."

❖ IMPATIENCE - *James 5:7-8* - "Be patient, therefore, brothers, until the coming of the Lord. See how the farmer waits for the precious fruit of the earth, being patient about it, until it receives the early and the late rains. You also, be patient. Establish your hearts, for the coming of the Lord is at hand."

❖ INSECURITIES - *I Samuel 16:7* - "But the LORD said to Samuel, Do not consider his appearance or his height, for I have rejected him. The LORD does not look at the things man looks at. Man looks at the outward appearance, but the LORD looks at the heart."

❖ INSTANT GRATIFICATION - *Isaiah 40:31* - "But they who wait for the Lord shall renew their strength; they shall mount up with wings like eagles; they shall run and not be weary; they shall walk and not faint."

❖ JEALOUSY - *James 3:14-15* - "But if you have bitter jealousy and selfish ambition in your hearts, do not boast and be false to the truth. This is not the wisdom that comes down from above, but is earthly, unspiritual, demonic."

❖ LACK OF FAITH - *Matthew 21:21* - "And Jesus answered them, "Truly, I say to you, if you have faith and do not doubt, you will not only do what has been done to the fig tree, but even if you say to this mountain, 'Be taken up and thrown into the sea,' it will happen."

❖ LAZINESS - *Proverbs 13:4* - "The soul of the sluggard craves and gets nothing, but the soul of the diligent is made fat."

❖ LOOKING FOR LOVE - *I Corinthians 13:4-8* - "Love is patient and kind; love does not envy or boast; it is not arrogant or rude. It does not insist on its own way; it is not irritable or resentful; it does not rejoice at wrongdoing, but rejoices with the truth. Love bears all things, believes all things, hopes all things, and endures all things. Love never ends. As for prophecies, they will pass away; as for tongues, they will cease; as for knowledge, it will pass away."

❖ LOW SELF-ESTEEM - *Song of Solomon 4:7* - "You are altogether beautiful, my love; there is no flaw in you."

❖ LUST - *I Corinthians 6:18* - "Flee from sexual immorality. Every other sin a person commits is outside the body, but the sexually immoral person sins against his own body."

❖ LYING - *Colossians 3:9* - "Do not lie to one another, for you have put off the old self with its habits."

❖ MATERIAL POSSESSIONS - *Mark 8:36* - "For what does it profit a man to gain the whole world, and forfeit his soul?"

❖ MENTAL ABUSE - *III John 1:2* - "Beloved, I pray that all may go well with you and that you may be in good health, as it goes well with your soul."

❖ MOLESTATION - *Matthew 6:14-15* - "For if you forgive others their trespasses, your heavenly Father will also forgive you, but if you do not forgive others their trespasses, neither will your Father forgive your trespasses."

❖ NEGATIVE INFLUENCES - *I Corinthians 15:33*- "Do not be deceived: "Bad company corrupts good morals."

❖ NERVOUSNESS - *I Peter 5:7* - "Casting all your anxieties on him, because he cares for you."

❖ NO VISION - *Habakkuk 2:2* - "And the LORD answered me, and said, write the vision, and make *it* plain upon tables, that he may run that readeth it."

❖ OBSESSIVE BEHAVIORS - *II Corinthians 10:4-5* - "For the weapons of our warfare are not of the flesh but have divine power to destroy strongholds. We destroy arguments and every lofty opinion raised against the knowledge of God, and take every thought captive to obey Christ."

- ❖ OTHERS PERECEPTION - *Galatians 1:10* - "For am I now seeking the approval of man, or of God? Or am I trying to please man? If I were still trying to please man, I would not be a servant of Christ."

- ❖ OURSELVES - *Luke 9:28* - "And he said to all, "If anyone would come after me, let him deny himself and take up his cross daily and follow me."

- ❖ OVER EATING - *Proverbs 25:27* - "It is not good to eat much honey, nor is it glorious to seek one's own glory."

- ❖ OVER THINKING - *Philippians 4:6-9* - "Do not be anxious about anything, but in everything by prayer and supplication with thanksgiving let your requests be made known to God. And the peace of God, which surpasses all understanding, will guard your hearts and your minds in Christ Jesus. Finally, brothers, whatever is true, whatever is honorable, whatever is just, whatever is pure, whatever is lovely, whatever is commendable, if there is any excellence, if there is anything worthy of praise, think about these things. What you have learned and received and heard and seen in me—practice these things, and the God of peace will be with you."

- ❖ OVER WORKED - *Psalm 127:1-5* - "Except the LORD build the house, they labour in vain that build it: except the LORD keep the city, the watchman waketh but in vain. It is vain for you to rise up early, to sit up late, to eat the bread of sorrows: for so he giveth his beloved sleep. Lo, children are an heritage of the LORD: and the fruit of the womb is his reward. As arrows are in the hand of a mighty man; so are children of the youth. Happy is the man that hath his quiver full of them: they shall not be ashamed, but they shall speak with the enemies in the gate."

❖ PARANOIA - *II Timothy 1:7* - "For God hath not given us the spirit of fear; but of power, and of love, and of a sound mind."

❖ PAST HURTS - *Ephesians 4:31* - "Let all bitterness and wrath and anger and clamor and slander be put away from you, along with all malice."

❖ PEER PRESSURE - *Exodus 23:2* - "You shall not follow the masses in doing evil, nor shall you testify in a dispute so as to turn aside after a multitude in order to pervert justice;"

❖ PERFECTION - *Ecclesiastes 7:20* - "Surely there is not a righteous man on earth who does good and never sins."

❖ PHOBIAS - *II Timothy 1:7* - "For God hath not given us the spirit of fear; but of power, and of love, and of a sound mind."

❖ PHYSICAL ABUSE - *I Corinthians 6:19-20* - "Or do you not know that your body is a temple of the Holy Spirit within you, whom you have from God? You are not your own, for you were bought with a price. So glorify God in your body."

❖ PLEASING MAN - *Psalm 118:8* - "It is better to trust in the Lord: then to put confidence in man."

❖ POOR MULTI-TASKING - *Ecclesiastes 4:6* - "Better is a handful of quietness than two hands full of toil and a striving after wind."

❖ POOR QUALITY OF LIFE - *III John 1:2* - "Beloved, I wish above all things that thou mayest prosper and be in health, even as thy soul prospereth."

❖ PORNOGRAPHY - *Psalm 119:9-10* - "How can a young man keep his way pure? By guarding it according to your word. With my whole heart I seek you; let me not wander from your commandments!"

❖ PRE-MARITAL SEX - *I Thessalonians 4:3-5* - "For this is the will of God, your sanctification: that you abstain from sexual immorality; that each one of you know how to control his own body in holiness and honor, not in the passion of lust like the Gentiles who do not know God;"

❖ PREJUDICE - *James 2:1-26* - "My brothers, show no partiality as you hold the faith in our Lord Jesus Christ, the Lord of glory. For if a man wearing a gold ring and fine clothing comes into your assembly, and a poor man in shabby clothing also comes in, and if you pay attention to the one who wears the fine clothing and say, "You sit here in a good place," while you say to the poor man, "You stand over there," or, "Sit down at my feet," have you not then made distinctions among yourselves and become judges with evil thoughts? Listen, my beloved brothers, has not God chosen those who are poor in the world to be rich in faith and heirs of the kingdom, which he has promised to those who love him?...."

❖ PRIDE - *Romans 12:3* - "For by the grace given to me I say to everyone among you not to think of himself more highly than he ought to think, but to think with sober judgment, each according to the measure of faith that God has assigned."

❖ PROCRASTINATION - *Proverbs 13:4* - "The soul of the sluggard craves and gets nothing, while the soul of the diligent is richly supplied."

❖ RAPE - *Psalm 9:9* - "The Lord is a stronghold for the oppressed, a stronghold in times of trouble."

❖ REBELLIOUS CHILDREN - *Proverbs 13:24* - "Whoever spares the rod hates his son, but he who loves him is diligent to discipline him."

❖ REJECTION - *Hebrews 4:15* - "For we do not have a High Priest Who is unable to understand and sympathize and have a shared feeling with our weaknesses and infirmities and liability to the assaults of temptation, but One Who has been tempted in every respect as we are, yet without sinning."

❖ RELATIONSHIPS - *II Corinthians 6:14* - "Do not be unequally yoked with unbelievers. For what partnership has righteousness with lawlessness? Or what fellowship has light with darkness?"

❖ RESENTMENT - *Luke 6:37* - "Judge not, and you will not be judged; condemn not, and you will not be condemned; forgive, and you will be forgiven;"

❖ SELF-GAIN - *Luke 9:25* - "What good is it for someone to gain the whole world, and yet lose or forfeit their very self."

❖ SELF PERCEPTION - *II Corinthians 5:17* - "Therefore, if anyone is in Christ, he is a new creation. The old has passed away; behold, the new has come."

❖ SELF PITY - *II Kings 19:4-15* - "While pitying himself, Elijah asks for death, saying, It is enough! Now LORD, take my life, for I am no better than my fathers!" His situation reveals several problems that can fatigue and erode our attitudes: He presumes the outcome, focuses on the problem and himself, and becomes physically exhausted. God provides the solutions to alleviate self-pity: Pray for God's help, rest, find a new focus and new expectations, repent of sins, and take obedient action. When Elijah crawls into his shell, God commands him to get up and get moving. He wants Elijah to choose godly action based on obedience rather than inaction based on his emotions. Genuine repentance and a clear view of our true condition, not a distorted one, fights self-pity."

❖ SELF-RIGHTEOUSNESS - *Matthew 7:1-5* - "Judge not, that ye be not judged. For with what judgment ye judge, ye shall be judged: and with what measure ye mete, it shall be measured to you again. And why beholdest thou the mote that is in thy brother's eye, but considerest not the beam that is in thine own eye? Or how wilt thou say to thy brother, Let me pull out the mote out of thine eye; and, behold, a beam is in thine own eye? Thou hypocrite, first cast out the beam out of thine own eye; and then shalt thou see clearly to cast out the mote out of thy brother's eye."

❖ SERVING THE CHURCH - *Galatians 6:10* - "So then, as we have opportunity, let us do good to everyone, and especially to those who are of the household of faith."

❖ SICKNESS - *Psalm 107:20* - "He sent out his word and healed them, and delivered them from their destruction."

- ❖ SKIN COLOR - *Psalm 139:14* - "I will praise thee; for I am fearfully and wonderfully made: marvelous are thy works; and that my soul knoweth right well."

- ❖ STEREOTYPES - *John 7:24* - "Judge not according to the appearance, but judge righteous judgment."

- ❖ SUBSTANCE ABUSE - *Romans 12:1* - "I appeal to you therefore, brothers, by the mercies of God, to present your bodies as a living sacrifice, holy and acceptable to God, which is your spiritual worship."

- ❖ SUICIDE- *1 Corinthians 6:20* - "You were bought at a price. Therefore honor God with your bodies."

- ❖ SUPERFICIAL LOVE - *John 13:34* - "A new command I give you: Love one another. As I have loved you, so you must love one another."

- ❖ TELEVISION - *Colossians 3:2* - "Set your minds on things that are above, not on things that are on earth."

- ❖ TEMPTATION - *1 Corinthians 10:13* - "No test or temptation that comes your way is beyond the course of what others have had to face. All you need to remember is that God will never let you down; he'll never let you be pushed past your limit; he'll always be there to help you come through it."

- ❖ TEXTURE OF YOUR HAIR - *Psalm 139:14* - "I will praise thee; for I am fearfully and wonderfully made: marvelous are thy works; and that my soul knoweth right well."

- ❖ THE AMERICAN DREAM - *II Peter 1:3* - "His divine power has granted to us all things that pertain to life and godliness, through the knowledge of him who called us to his own glory and excellence."

❖ THE FEAR OF DYING - *John 3:16* - "For God so loved the world, that he gave his only Son, that whoever believes in him should not perish but have eternal life." *I Corinthians 5:22* - "For as in Adam all die, so also in Christ shall all be made alive."

❖ THE INTERNET - *Colossians 3:2* - "Set your minds on things that are above, not on things that are on earth."

❖ THE MEDIA - *Colossians 3:2* - "Set your minds on things that are above, not on things that are on earth."

❖ THE OUTCOME OF A SITUATION - *Matthew 6:34* - "Therefore do not worry about tomorrow, for tomorrow will worry about itself. Each day has enough trouble of its own."

❖ THINGS THAT YOU CAN'T CHANGE - *Philippians 4:11* - "I have learned in whatever situation I am to be content."

❖ TIREDNESS - *Galatians 6:9* - "So let's not get tired of doing what is good. At just the right time we will reap a harvest of blessing if we don't give up."

❖ TOO MUCH RESPONSIBILITY - *Psalm 127:2* - "It is in vain that you rise up early and go late to rest, eating the bread of anxious toil; for he gives to his beloved sleep."

❖ UNCOMPASSIONATE - *Ephesians 4:32* - "Be kind to one another, tenderhearted, forgiving one another, as God in Christ forgave you."

❖ UNFORGIVENESS - *II Corinthians 2:10-11* - "Anyone whom you forgive, I also forgive. Indeed, what I have forgiven, if I have forgiven anything, has been for your sake in the presence of Christ, so that we would not be outwitted by Satan; for we are not ignorant of his designs."

❖ UNFULFILLMENT - *Isaiah 55:2* - "Why spend money on what is not bread, and your labor on what does not satisfy? Listen, listen to me, and eat what is good and you will delight in the richest of fare."

❖ UNPRODUCTIVE BUSYNESS - *Titus 3:14* - "Our people must learn to devote themselves to doing what is good, in order to provide for urgent needs and not live unproductive lives."

❖ UNRESOLVED ISSUES - *Romans 6:12* - "Let not sin therefore reign in your mortal body, to make you obey its passions."

❖ UNWORTHINESS - *Philippians 4:19* - "I can do all things through him who strengthens me."

❖ VERBAL ABUSE - *Proverbs 22:24* - "Make no friendship with a man given to anger, nor go with a wrathful man."

❖ WEIGHT - *I Corinthians 6:19* - "Do you not know that your bodies are temples of the Holy Spirit, who is in you, whom you have received from God? You are not your own;"

❖ WORRY - *Matthew 6:25-34* - "Therefore I tell you, do not worry about your life, what you will eat or drink; or about your body, what you will wear. Is not life more than food, and the body more than clothes? Look at the birds of the air; they do not sow or reap or store away in barns, and yet your heavenly Father feeds them. Are you not much more valuable than they? Can any one of you by worrying add a single hour to your life? And why do you worry about clothes? See how the flowers of the field grow. They do not labor or spin. Yet I tell you that not even Solomon in all his splendor was dressed like one of these. If that is how God clothes the grass of the field, which is here today and tomorrow is thrown into the fire, will he not much more clothe you—you of little faith? So do not worry, saying, 'What shall we eat?' or 'What shall we drink?' or 'What shall we wear?' For the pagans run after all these things, and your heavenly Father knows that you need them. But seek first his kingdom and his righteousness, and all these things will be given to you as well. Therefore do not worry about tomorrow, for tomorrow will worry about itself. Each day has enough trouble of its own."

❖ DISTRACTIONS - *1 Corinthians 7:34-35* - "So he is pulled in two directions. Unmarried women and women who have never been married worry only about pleasing the Lord, and they keep their bodies and minds pure. But a married woman worries about the things of this world, because she wants to please her husband. What I am saying is for your own good—it isn't to limit your freedom. I want to help you to live right and to love the Lord above all else."
Psalm 1:2 - "But they delight in the law of the Lord, meditating on it day and night."
Psalm 119:15 - "I will study your commandments and reflect on your ways."
Proverbs 5:1 - "My son, pay attention to my wisdom, turn your ear to my words of insight"

Chapter IX

Refocus, Restart & Readjust

Chapter IX

Refocus, Restart & Readjust

After being distracted so long by so many distractions how do you refocus, restart and readjust to be being focused again. Let's take a look at a passage of scripture in Mathew 14-22-33 which declares:

[22] Immediately Jesus made the disciples get into the boat and go on ahead of him to the other side, while he dismissed the crowd. [23] After he had dismissed them, he went up on a mountainside by himself to pray. Later that night, he was there alone, [24] and the boat was already a considerable distance from land, buffeted by the waves because the wind was against it.

[25] Shortly before dawn Jesus went out to them, walking on the lake. [26] When the disciples saw him walking on the lake, they were terrified. "It's a ghost," they said, and cried out in fear.

[27] But Jesus immediately said to them: "Take courage! It is I. Don't be afraid."

[28] "Lord, if it's you," Peter replied, "tell me to come to you on the water."

[29] "Come," he said.

Then Peter got down out of the boat, walked on the water and came toward Jesus. [30] But when he saw the wind, he was afraid and, beginning to sink, cried out, "Lord, save me!"

[31] Immediately Jesus reached out his hand and caught him. "You of little faith," he said, "why did you doubt?"

[32] And when they climbed into the boat, the wind died down. [33] Then those who were in the boat worshiped him, saying, "Truly you are the Son of God."

This particular passage of scripture is about a disciple named Peter who initially asks Jesus to bid him to come and walk on water. Peter walks out of the boat on the "Rhema" word that's proceeding out of the mouth of his master Jesus and begins to walk on the water. At this particular time he's focused on the one that bids him to come. However in the process of him focusing on the master, a distraction appeared in the form of the wind. The Bible states that Peter saw the wind and he was afraid. As I pondered on the text I said, "Wait one minute! You can't see the wind-the wind is invisible." However, you can feel and see the effects of the wind. I liken this wind to the spirit of distraction because many times we can't see the distraction but we can defiantly see how it affects our lives. The moment Peter saw the effects that the wind had on him and his surroundings, the distraction of fear appeared and the bible declares to us that Peter began to sink. This sinking could have been deadly and maybe even fatal, but there was one present that was the master of the sea and of the wind and his name is Jesus. Peter understands that Jesus is his life line and source so he cries out for help. In response to his plea for help Jesus addresses Peter's low faith and his distraction of doubt. It was then and only then that Peter refocused, restarted and readjusted. Peter had to put his eyes back on his master the one that bade him to come in the first place and not on the distractions that presented themselves at the moment. He had to start all over again and revisit the fact that this same Jesus was also standing on top of the water without sinking and if He was not afraid and doubtful and if He was not fearful Peter shouldn't be either. Peter's way of readjusting and recovering after being distracted by the effects of the wind was to clearly put his trust and confidence in Jesus. He had taken his eyes off of Jesus and put them on his surroundings and he suddenly began to sink.

So as it is in the natural it is in the spiritual, we must recognize that the moment we spiritually take our focus off of Jesus and his word and are pulled away by the distractions in our lives, we begin to sink but if we just refocus, readjust and restart the God that we serve will show us just how much he loves us. The hymnist pens an old hymn of the church:

I was sinking deep in sin, far from the peaceful shore,
Very deeply stained within, sinking to rise no more,
But the Master of the sea, heard my despairing cry,
From the waters lifted me, now safe am I.

Love lifted me! Love lifted me!
When nothing else could help
Love lifted me!

Souls in danger look above, Jesus completely saves,
He will lift you by His love, out of the angry waves.
He's the Master of the sea, billows His will obey,
He your Savior wants to be, be saved today.

Love lifted me! Love lifted me!
When nothing else could help
Love lifted me!

    Hallelujah! Love lifted us from some horrible pits and some bad situations. It sometimes appeared that we were going to be overtaken, but by the grace and mercy of God we are still standing today. God gives us enough strength to refocus, restart and readjust. Today is your day, beloved, to refocus your attention on God and the things that matter. It is your day, beloved, to restart something that you started and walked away from. It's your day, to restart that which God started in you. For he that has begun to do a good work in you shall perform it until the day of Jesus Christ. You have been hindered long enough; now it's your time to finish. The Bible says the race is not given to the swift nor to the strong but to him who endures until the end. You may not have come in first place, but with the help of God you finished what you started. You must remember that God has the ability to help you finish what He started. There are some things that you began years ago that have been left undone, but today is your day to get up, restart and finish. Today is your day, beloved, to readjust and get back in the race that you once ran. It's your time to readjust the way you look at your life and refocus your lens of perception and see that which lies ahead of you. For Paul declares in Philippians 3:12:14, "Not that I have already attained, or am already perfected; he says but I press on, that I may lay hold of that for which Christ Jesus has also laid hold of me, he says, Brethren, I do not count myself to have apprehended; but one thing *I do,* forgetting those things which are behind and reaching forward to those things which are ahead, I press toward the goal for the prize of the upward call of God in Christ Jesus."

It's time for you to readjust, stop looking at the distractions that are behind you and press forward to the prize and the mark of the higher calling that is in Christ Jesus. Hallelujah! You must get in the press; it's going to take some endurance and some strength, but it's time for you to get in the press. It's not going to be easy, but get in the press. There will be some obstacles that get in your way, but stay in the press. There may be some people that try to block you, but stay in the press. There may be some situations that arise in your life, but stay in the press, for you must know that God is with thee and he is well able to keep you. It's your time to refocus, restart and readjust because your life is better when it's undistracted.

Chapter X

Life Is Better Undistracted

Chapter X
Life Is Better Undistracted

In order for you to live an undistracted life, you must first know your purpose. You must know your reason for being, the reason why you were created and what you will contribute to the earth before leaving it. An undistracted life is a life that has meaning, it's a life lived on purpose, it's a life lived intentionally. It's a life lived with the consciousness that your time here on earth is precious, and that time lost will never be able to be regained.

An undistracted life is a life that has a greater appreciation for the things most people take for granted. Take for example the number of breaths that one takes every minute; studies have shown that the average adult inhales and exhales between 16-20 times per minute, many times without even realizing it. Have you ever counted your breaths, or intentionally taken time out to appreciate this very source of life called oxygen? Have you ever really thought about the air that we breathe and the ability of your lungs to inflate and deflate sending oxygen to your brain so that you can live? My brother or my sister, if you were distracted, like me, your answer, like mine, is no. Have you ever noticed or taken time out in a quiet place just to listen to the beating of your heart? It is said that the normal human heart beats over 100,000 times in a day, 35 million times in a year, and 2.6 billion in an average lifetime. How many days have gone by that we have taken the beating of our hearts for granted, never considering that at any moment, if our heart decides to stop beating we would cease to exist? An undistracted life assumes sensitivity to the things often overlooked or the things that are usually taken for granted.

Beloved, we can become so distracted by the noise in our lives that the vital entities that keep us alive go unnoticed, and if they ever stop functioning properly or if there is a limited supply of it we would cease to exist. I often pondered the fact of how we as humans can give so much attention to our distractions, our problems, our situations, or our circumstances, and ignore or miss the meaningful things in our lives.

Recently, I was searching the web and came across an article that stated that the earth would be without the sun for approximately 14 days. I immediately knew that this had to be a hoax, but in that moment my mind shifted and I thought, just what if the earth was without the sun for 14 days. How many times did we see the sun rise and set and not appreciate it? From that moment on I have decided to appreciate the beauty of how God allows the sun to rise in the east and set in the west, even on cloudy days, and just because we can't see it doesn't mean that it's not happening.

An undistracted life is sensitive and appreciative to its God, who is the very source and foundation of life itself. It's a life that understands that it is in God that you live; it is in God that you move and it is in God that you have your very being. It's a life that understands that God is not on some far off planet and can't be reached and doesn't care about you but He's a God who comes nigh unto us and constantly interacts in the affairs of men. It's a life that understands that God is with you always. He's with you even when you didn't even know that He was with you. He is with you in the good times, he is with you in the bad times, and He is available when you need Him.

An undistracted person is sensitive to the leading of the Holy Spirit because they understand that the Holy Spirit's job is to lead and guide them into all truth. They understand that they can't make a decision on a situation whether big or small without involving God and seeking His advice. When you get to the place of being undistracted, you can hear God clearly, you can see things better, and you can make "God choices" instead of "good choices".

There were many times that Jesus withdrew himself from the masses and retreated to the mountainside or to the wilderness to pray and to get away from the distractions. An undistracted life is one of prayer, and if life is going to get better beloved, we must consistently withdraw from our distractions and develop a prayer life with our God. Another one of my favorite authors is Pastor Mark Batterson, who states in his book, *The Circle Maker,* that "The greatest tragedy in life is the prayers that go unanswered because they go unasked." For many of us, the distractions of our lives have hindered us from praying. It seems as if there just isn't enough time in our busy day to pray to our God, so therefore, we have not articulated in words that which we desire God to do for us.

Prayer is a two way communication between you and God. It's a conversation with God that requires listening and speaking. There are times that you'll have to leave the noise, deny the invitation and even walk away from some people to listen and hear from Jesus. He speaks in the stillness of the night, he speaks through the pages of the book, he speaks through the consciousness of our minds, and he speaks through the situations and circumstances that have presented themselves to us. Believe me! If you just walk away from the distractions in your life you will hear him when he speaks.

I have learned, in my place of being undistracted, the beauty of life. I have learned to enjoy the sounds of birds chirping in the morning, the splashing of water on the rocks of the sea, and the whistling of the wind through the air. I've learned to take heed to Godly counsel and wisdom that will save me some heartaches and heartbreaks. I have learned how to look back at my trials and tribulations and realize that I was a survivor the moment God brought me out. I have learned that in whatever situation I may find myself, I am the victor instead of the victim.

When you get in the place of being undistracted, you can get more done in three days that you have not gotten done in three years. All God needed was your attention. The Lord declares, "Come up hither!" so that he may show us and tell us things that eye have not seen nor have ear heard neither have it entered into the hearts of men the things that God has prepared for those who love him. When you are in need of direction, you must consult Jesus Christ, for it is he who will unfold his divine purpose and plan for your life. God desires for us to depend on him, he loves it when we need his assistance.

To enjoy life undistracted, you must set aside a time in your day that's devoted to God. In the early part of the fall I made a visit to Washington, DC, and decided to visit the Lincoln Memorial and the Pool of Reflection on the National Mall. I walked from the Washington Monument, past the World War II Memorial, alongside the pool, and up the steps to the Lincoln Memorial, at night. At night there were fewer distractions, and so I had an opportunity to live in the moment. I left the Lincoln Memorial and I stood at the tip of the pool of reflection facing the Washington Monument. It was there that I received an awesome revelation: the power to reflect.

Reflecting on your life and how far God has brought you is vital to appreciating where you are today. Many times when we are distracted there isn't enough time in our busy schedules to reflect. We must learn to not only reflect on our lives, but to reflect on our day, so that we can acknowledge the goodness of the Lord in our lives. As I stood at the tip of the Reflecting Pool I saw a mirror of the Washington Monument which was so far away but looked as if I could grab it. I appreciated, at that very moment, the God given ability to reflect, the ability to look back and appreciate how far we have come. Beloved, it is your time to live in the moment, to appreciate your life, to become aware of the blessings in your life, and to live an undistracted life.

Chapter XI

No More Distractions

Chapter XI

No More Distractions

We must get to the place where we make up our minds that we must be focused and undistracted. I dare you to declare, "I refuse to be distracted. I refuse to allow the distractions of my life to delay me. I refuse to lose my faith. I refuse to be stagnated. I refuse to lose my hope. I refuse to stop showing love. I refuse to be defeated. I refuse to be depressed. I refuse to live an unfulfilled and a distracted life." You must make the conscious decision today, that you will no longer entertain the distractions that life has sent your way. That this is the last straw, that enough is enough and you must get focused.

Unfortunately, beloved, we have wasted so much time and energy on our distractions; they have caused us much pain, heartbreak, money, misery and time. But today, I dare you to declare out of your own mouth that "I must cut some people off, delete some phone numbers, change my phone number, let some things go, apologize to someone, and begin to eliminate many of the distractions that have held me bound for so long and have delayed my destiny." My brother or my sister, if you have to move to another state or move across town it's imperative that you do so, because God needs your attention. Today is your day, beloved, and you must be determined about your future and fight to reclaim your focus. You must be determined like Jesus, who kept his eyes on the prize. You have the rest of your life before you and a rewarding task and assignment to fulfill. When you get to the place where you can declare "No More Distractions!" that's when the book that you started writing years ago can get completed, the business that you desire can be in operation, that calling that you have been running from for years can finally be answered and accepted, that degree that you started can be finished, that million dollar idea can be manifested and your dreams can be fulfilled. There are people waiting, whose very lives depend on you becoming who God has intended for you to be. It is much bigger than you and I; there are those who are connected to our destinies that need us to stay focused so that they can become who God has created them to be and those who are divinely connected to us, are going to make it because we made it.

Let's take a look at a person in the Bible whose life exemplifies an attitude and position of "No More Distractions." and of course that person is the God-Man, Jesus Christ. Through the scriptures we can find instances where Jesus overcame distractions. While here on earth, Jesus was very focused and sensitive to his mission. It was very important for Him to keep focused. I liken it to the importance of a surgeon performing open heart surgery on a patient, how it's imperative that the surgeon keep focus and eliminate most, if not all of the distractions that may hinder the successful outcome for the patient. Just like the surgeon, Jesus has an awareness and sensitivity to the task that has been laid before Him. He declared often throughout the New Testament scriptures, that His days were short and how He was sent to do the will of His father. However, He knew that He came to earth as a suffering servant, the kinsmen redeemer, the sacrificial lamb that was slain before the foundation of the world and His focus never became distorted.

John 3:16, states "For God so loved the world that he gave his only begotten Son, that whosoever believeth in him should not perish, but have everlasting life. It then shifts and

John 3:17 read, "For God sent not his Son into the world to condemn the world; but that the world through him might be saved." Jesus' assignment was cleared up and made known unto us in these two verses. One of the main reasons that Jesus was sent to the earth was because God loved the WORLD. God wanted everyone in the world to have an opportunity to partake in everlasting life.

It was this Jesus that was sent from heaven who is also referred to as the second Adam, who came to undo what the first Adam messed up in the Garden of Eden, by being distracted. As we search the scriptures there were many things, people, situations, and distractions that Jesus encountered before making it to Calvary. There were many things that came to distract Him from His purpose. The first instance was the premature death edict given by King Herod, that all first born male babies were to be killed, and that was to include Jesus. By divine intervention He escaped and continued to grow into His destiny. Throughout Jesus' mission towards His assignment there were many accusations, betrayals, and evil spirits that came to distract him from His purpose, but Jesus was persistent, for He knew that our lives depended on Him staying focused. Jesus knew that the weight of all creation lies within His hands and that the task is important. He's the one the prophets spoke about. He is the one that was there in the beginning and He is the long awaited king. However, the very ones that He came to die for rejected and despised Him, they didn't even esteem Him. They were the very ones that hailed, "Crucify Him." But Jesus, did not allow that to distract him from his assignment.

There was an instance where the devil came to tempt Jesus while He was in the midst of praying and fasting. This was just another ploy to break His focus. Jesus knew how to combat the distractions of the enemy by using the word of God and guess what, the enemy had to adhere. It was later that Jesus finds himself in the garden of Gethsemane, sweating drops of blood, in distress at the thought of what He was to take on and experience for mankind. There was a wrestle between His will versus the will of His father and at one point he pleads with His father to remove the cup from Him and to let it pass, only moments later realizing that not even His will can distract Him from his purpose. He later retreats and declares, "Father not my will but yours be done." and He regains His focus.

Jesus was betrayed by one of the very disciples that He chose to follow Him, for 30 pieces of silver (the cost of a slave), but that still was not enough to distract Him from His purpose. He was dragged through the streets of Jerusalem, taken before an unrighteous court, whipped, spat upon, humiliated, and criticized. His body was in pain and in agony but all of that was not enough to distract Him from fulfilling His task and assignment on the earth. He was laughed at, mocked, betrayed, denied, and put on public display, but Jesus never allowed any of those things to distract Him. This Jesus was so exhausted that He required the assistance of an African man whose name was Thomas of Cyrene, to carry the cross the rest of the way. They drove six inch spikes through His wrists severing the nerves in His wrists sending painful shocks up and down His arms, but, that was still not enough to distract Jesus from His destiny.

They whipped Him 39 times upon His back; they placed a crown of thorns upon His head and labeled Him the King of the Jews, leaving this Jesus a bloody mess. He's slowly dying from dehydration and asphyxiation and the Bible clearly states that He had ten thousand angels at His disposal and could have requested their assistance but He chose to endure the cross because He didn't even want the pain in His body and what was happening to Him physically to distract Him from His purpose. Jesus kept focus on His mission and assignment having felt forsaken because this was the very first time that He felt the absence of His father. It was as if His father had stood afar off and watched as His son took on the sins of the entire world that He was sent to die for. Can you just imagine what took place at that very moment, that even the sun hid its face from Him? Honestly, that would have been my climax that would have been my breaking point; however, I'm so glad that Jesus is not like me. He had focus, He had persistence, He had stamina, He had endurance, and He had a clear view of His destiny.

When He had overcome all that had come to distract Him from His assignment, He declared, "father into thy hands I commend my spirit," and He gave up the ghost, and the soldiers came to break His legs to speed up the death process. The scriptures declare, "They break not His legs." For not a bone in His body was broken. For this truly fulfilled the Old Testament scriptures. He declared that no man took His life, but He willfully laid it down.

But that's not the end of the story. This was Jesus' entry into Hell, for this death process gave Him a foothold into the domain of Hell where the devil held power. For there were those who were held captive in Paradise (a section in Hell) who needed to be liberated, and not even death could distract Him because He defeats death, He defeats hell, and He defeats the grave. For He triumphantly rises on the third day with all power in His hands, thereby leading the captives out of captivity and liberating those who were bound in Paradise. He spends 40 days on the earth in His glorified body and before He bids them farewell, He declares that they must stay in Jerusalem and wait and pray for the comforter to come. During His ascension into heaven His disciples are standing, gazing as their father, teacher, rabbi, and savior fades away in the clouds. It was the angel who declares to them, "Why, do you stand here gazing, for this same Jesus that was taken up will come back the same way." Jesus assumes His position at the right hand of the father, receiving power and authority. This position is not an actual place but a role that he takes. For He and His father are one, for the flesh of Jesus has become the image of God, and God fully embodies Jesus, and sits on the mercy seat in heaven.

For God is still the God of justice and when we sin, Jesus, the image stands in the gap for us and makes intercession for us. That's when God looks down upon his hands and sees the holes caused by the nails on Calvary, and mercy and grace are applied to our lives. Oh, how grateful I am that Jesus didn't give into the distractions that he encountered on his road to destiny; that he had you and me on his mind.

As you read the last couple of paragraphs of this book, I have something to reveal to you: I want you to know that the biggest distraction mankind could ever encounter is a life without God. Many have tried to go through this life without him and have found themselves living unfulfilled lives. We have tried everything else, we have tried everyone else, but still our lives have been in shambles. If you haven't accepted Jesus as your personal savior, today is your day and God has your attention. If you have already accepted him I applaud your acceptance of him, and I pray that God continues to bless your life tremendously.

For those of you who have found yourselves in a backslidden state, or you desire to accept him today, I would like to extend the plan of salvation to you. Romans 10:9

states, "That if thou shalt confess with thy mouth the Lord Jesus, and shalt believe in thine heart that God hath raised Him from the dead, thou shalt be saved." So the first order of business is to totally surrender and as a sign of you surrendering, lift both hands as an indication to God that you are inviting Him in and that you want Him in your life. Next, I want you to put your sins at the forefront of your mind. I'm talking about those things that you know you have done wrong and in your own way begin to ask God for forgiveness. Confess your sins to God; make all of your ways known to God. Illuminate every dark corner of your being. You must mean it from the bottom of your heart. You must believe in your heart that Jesus lived, that He died, and that on the third day He rose again just for you. In order to go any further you must first believe it. I caution you not to just do this because you feel pressured but accept Him because you really believe. You must now tell Jesus that you accept Him as your personal Lord and Savior. The Bible declares that now you are saved. Now this is the part of the plan where I get excited, I want you to open your mouth and denounce Satan, with power and authority. I dare you to declare: "Satan, I don't belong to you I belong to Jesus Christ!" Now give our God your best praise.

The steps above are just the first couple of steps to your salvation. For Peter says in Acts 2:38 that, "We are to repent [to turn away from sin when it comes], and be baptized [be fully immersed into a watery grave] every one of you in the name of Jesus Christ [it's the only name given amongst men to be saved] for the remission of sins, [for the forgiveness of our sins] and ye shall receive the gift of the Holy Ghost [the indwelling of God himself followed by the initial evidence of tongues]."

And it shall come to pass afterward, that I will pour out my spirit upon all flesh; and your sons and your daughters shall prophesy, your old men shall dream dreams, your young men shall see visions. -Joel 2:28

And lastly you must find a Bible believing church that teaches and preaches the truth and be natured in the word of God. Beloved, Remember, "No More Distractions!" and that you *can* live un-distracted. Peace be unto you from God our Father and the Lord Jesus Christ.

Close the book and lift your hands! Because our God used all of this just to get your attention.

No More
DISTRACTIONS!
Peace & Blessings

-Greg Johnson

THE GHANA PROJECT
Missions

PRAY FOR THOSE AROUND THE WORLD

THANK YOU FOR PURCHASING THIS BOOK 10% OF ALL PROCEEDS FROM THIS BOOK WILL BE SENT TO HELP THOSE IN GHANA, AFRICA.

"BUT YOU WILL RECEIVE POWER WHEN THE HOLY SPIRIT HAS COME UPON YOU, AND YOU WILL BE MY WITNESSES IN JERUSALEM AND IN ALL JUDEA AND SAMARIA, AND TO THE END OF THE EARTH." - ACTS 1:8

SIGN UP & RECIEVE THE
Daily
EXHORTATION
"Expecting the Harvest." -Matt 9:37

Sign Up Today By visiting
http://www.gregdjohnson.net/
daily-exhortation/

or by visiting us on:

/dailyexhortation

Minister
Greg Johnson

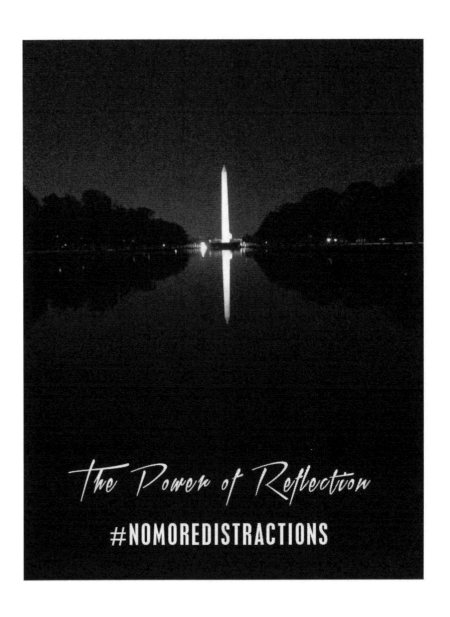

Notes

Made in the USA
Middletown, DE
08 February 2015